1

T

from its foundations. The lost lake
crumbling in the hands of brickmakers,
the floor of the ravine where light lies broken
with the memory of rivers. All the winters
stored in that geologic
garden. Dinosaurs sleep in the subway
at Bloor and Shaw, a bed of bones
under the rumbling track. The storm
that lit the city with the voltage
of spring, when we were eighteen
on the clean earth. The ferry ride in the rain,
wind wet with wedding music and everything that
sings in the carbon of stone and bone
like a page of love, wind-lost from a hand, unread.

Anne Michaels is an award-winning Toronto poet and novelist. She was a Giller Prize finalist in 1996, and won the 1997 Orange Prize for fiction for her novel *Fugitive Pieces*.

The Guide Book Team (in alphabetical order)

Key Editors: Rachel Dodds, Anna Gibson, Joan Miles, Sue Zielinski
Editing Team: Hans Burgschmidt, Sheila Conlin, Dianne Gibson, Kim Hume, Marion Joppe, Justin Lafontaine, Liz Martin, Wayne Roberts, Luke Wintjes
Writing Team: Rachel Dodds, Anna Gibson, Marion Joppe, Joan Miles, Bob Tremble, Sue Zielinski
Production Team: Rachel Dodds, Anna Gibson
Research Team: Rachel Dodds, Anna Gibson, Halim Abi Khaled, Joan Miles, Bob Tremble, Sue Zielinski
Template Design: John Canning, Communications, Graphics and Presentations Section, Urban Development Services, City of Toronto
Layout: Karen Birkemoe and Melissa McClellan
Copy Editor: Procedures Plus
Illustrations and hand drawn maps: Sari Spencer
Icons: Green Map Icons © Modern World Design 1999.

Bob Tremble (Lead Writer): Bob Tremble is a Toronto writer and social worker with a keen interest in community issues and a love of Canadian history. He was 1997 co-ordinator for the City of Toronto's Healthy City Week, celebrating achievements in the struggle for social, environmental, and economic harmony. He has managed projects in human services and has been published in both the academic and consumer press on mental health issues.

Sari Spencer (Illustrator): Sari Spencer was born and raised in North York, in Toronto. She attended York University (BFA) and the University of Toronto (BSc AAM). She has travelled extensively and has lived abroad for a few years. She currently works as a medical illustrator for Imagineering STA.

Acknowledgements (in alphabetical order)

We would like to express our heartfelt thanks to Jane Beecroft, Wendy Brawer, John Canning, Andrew Croft, Rosemary G. Hasner, Lynne Heise, Marusia Heney, Mark King, Josephine Lee Ka Ling, Monica Lo, Daya Lye, Beth McEwen, Vincenzo Pietropaolo, Daniella Remy, David Russo, Reg Scotland, Tanya Sokolowski, Michelle Stelter, John Sutton and the City of Toronto: Economic Development, Culture and Tourism, Graphics and Presentations, Museum and Heritage Services, Parks and Recreation and Urban Development Services.

Thanks to all the photographers and to all the people who helped us gather information and answer questions. Thanks also to Green Tourism Association members, board of directors, supporters and friends.

The development and production of this guide book was made possible by generous contributions from:

Human Resources Development Canada | Développement des ressources humaines Canada

TORONTO

Urban Development Services
Economic Development Partnership Program

THE ONTARIO TRILLIUM FOUNDATION
LA FONDATION TRILLIUM DE L'ONTARIO

ROYAL YORK
CANADIAN PACIFIC HOTELS

Table of Contents

The *OTHER* Guide to Toronto

Introduction

THIS IS NOT YOUR REGULAR GUIDE BOOK

Like the ***Other* Map of Toronto**, this guide was created by Toronto's Green Tourism Association to help you discover the true nature of Toronto, to serve as a companion on your journey to explore the greener side of the big city. It builds on the map, taking you deeper, and offering more juicy detail and practical information.

WHY AN *OTHER* GUIDE TO TORONTO?

Toronto has all the trappings of a mighty and impressive city: longest street in the world, highest tower in the world, hustle, bustle, big tall buildings, great convention facilities, lots to eat, arts and sports galore, sizzling night life. It's fully equipped with all the basics of a Boston, a New York, a Sydney, a Vienna or a Hong Kong. For this alone, it's well worth the visit.

But there's so much more. Especially for the growing community of people who are seeking to delve more deeply and to tread more lightly in their travels. Beneath and beyond the imposing Toronto skyscrapers lies a host of green oases, cultural gems, out of the way hang outs, and little known historical secrets. All of them bring you a little closer to Toronto's soul, and tempt you to surrender to the seduction of the city's gentler and wilder sides, to help you uncover its essence, its richness, and its magic.

Like so many good things in life, the "other" isn't always immediately apparent or easily accessible at first glance. This guide is an attempt to point you in the right direction, to offer you some great info, some practical tools and some general inspiration to set you on your own personal urban eco-tourism adventure.

WHY *URBAN* GREEN TOURISM?

Toronto gets over 21 million visitors every year, and on average they come back about 17 times. That can have a huge impact on Toronto's ecosystem. Just one car trip or styrofoam cup per visitor means 21 million more car rides or styrofoam cups every year. That many tourists can also have a big impact on our neighbourhoods and communities.

On the other hand, tourism is generally a good thing. Beyond inspiring interchange and understanding between people and among different cultures, it can also be pretty important to a city's economy. So we wanted to find a way to keep tourism strong and vibrant while at the same time making it greener, and perhaps even sparking ***new*** enterprises related to urban green tourism. After all, since eco-tourism is the fastest growing segment of the tourism industry world-wide, it makes sense to bring eco-tourism to the city, where tourism actually has just as big an impact, if not bigger.

At first, "urban eco-tourism" seems like a bit of an oxymoron. It's easy to think of cities as the "big smokes" that are polluting our pristine and fragile wildernesses and habitats. But as patterns of human settlement go, cities (and particularly compact cities) are about as efficient and ecological as you can get, especially when it comes to sharing services and resources and transportation amongst growing populations. In principle, in cities we can do more with less.

At the same time we know that cities don't have to feel crowded, or dirty, or frenetic, even when you have millions of residents augmented by millions of visitors each year. As we know from the world's great cities, it ***is*** possible to experience space and calm and nature in the midst of it all.

In fact, it seems that people are actually ***asking*** for urban ecotourism — whether they are living in Toronto or coming to visit. Tourism trends continue to move towards a desire for something different, something "REAL" (Rewarding, Enriching, Authentic, Learning).[1]

Toronto is an ideal place for developing and nurturing urban green tourism. We already have so many green and wonderful things to offer. Not only is Toronto one of the most multicultural cities in the world, we're also known for our high quality of life, our excellent transit system, our bicycle friendliness, and for our clean, safe streets and neighbourhoods.

In December 1999, Toronto was awarded what amounts to a "green oscar" for its efforts and success in recycling, tree planting, and overall 'greening' of the city. The award, given annually by The International Federation of Park and Recreation Administration, judges contestants on landscape enhancement, heritage management, environmentally sensitive practices, community involvement, and future planning.

Fortunately for the planet, the competition was tough. Cities around the world are increasingly considering environmental principles and practices as a necessary and integral part of their future planning and daily operations.

But very few cities have yet made a concerted connection between urban tourism and ecological health and renewal. It was through this little crack in the pavement that Toronto's Green Tourism Association sprouted up and grew. In 1993, a small and diverse group of Toronto folks saw the gap and started out on a mission:

To develop and cultivate a green tourism industry within the Toronto region, which is ecologically sound, fosters appreciation of, and respect for, diverse cultural and natural heritages, and strengthens local economies and communities.

Our main work is to try to provide greener options for tourists and for the tourism industry in the broadest of senses. So much more than just exploring the parks when you travel (although this is great), urban green tourism can include anything from cycling to the opera, to recycling your picnic containers, to getting involved in local arts and culture, to planting a tree, to eating locally grown organic food, to buying local environmental products, to adopting green practices in your tourism business. Green tourism runs the gamut.

So we carry out our mission first of all by promoting urban eco-tourism as an option. We also help new and existing businesses to go green and to benefit from going green.

For tourists and residents looking to explore the green side of Toronto, we have a green map, this guidebook, and a green tourism web site www.greentourism.on.ca. For businesses there are all sorts of perks and opportunities … joint promotions, a web listing, a newsletter, networking events, workshops, and more (For a list of our members, see page 155).

As support for our work grows, we are compiling increasing (and very scientific) evidence that urban green tourism is one of the most enjoyable forms of environmental action. We are thrilled to have you join us in our very important mission. Enjoy.

How to Use This Guide

We've attempted to organize the guide for quick and easy reference and cross-reference. We start at the beginning with some basic ideas about how to actually **practise** green tourism wherever you are.

Then we get you started with some resources for planning your trip to Toronto. In the interests of saving space and especially trees, rather than listing the details of absolutely everything, we refer you to other great guide books, weeklies and on-line resources for rounding out your research.

After that we go straight to the basics like how cold will it be, how hot will it be, what time will it be, where should I stay, and how should I get there?

The bulk of the book is called "Exploring the Other Side of Toronto". In an effort to follow a natural flow of exploration, we start downtown at Union Station, and move northward street by street as far as Bloor. With Yonge as the east-west dividing line, we follow each major street westward and then eastward. Once we hit Bloor, we go back to the source and explore the waterfront. Keeping with the water theme, we begin The Verticals by exploring the Humber River in the west, starting from the lake and moving north, then the Don River system in the east, also starting from the lake and moving north. Then we pick up where we left off at Bloor and go north on Yonge. Finally, we venture out to some "Gems of the Region" that take you a little farther afield (but they're worth it).

A few not-to-scale maps are provided to help you get the general lay of the land, and for each major area there's an "Essence" and a "Roots" section to help you get a sense of its character and evolution. Each area contains our recommended highlights as well as a list of great things to do, see and buy (listed in the order of how you would encounter them as you walk). We've highlighted mentions of our **members in bold green text**, and alphabetical listings at the back detail what they do and what they offer. If you get really keen, check the Resource Group section for ways to get actively involved in ecological action, sustainable transportation, or social justice activities.

This guide book is the result of many minds, experiences and suggestions by our Board of Directors, staff, friends and folks in the green and tourism communities. While we've tried to capture and share as much rich green content as we could find, we know there are jewels (perhaps even whole necklaces) that we've missed. Perhaps there are places where there is just too much information.

This is the first urban green tourism guide to Toronto (and possibly anywhere), so we welcome your comments and your stories on anything and everything about your experience with this guide and about your green tourism adventure in Toronto.

Approximately 17 trees are saved by recycling 1 tonne of newspaper. Recycling containers for newspaper, cans and bottles can be found throughout the city: silver boxes on sidewalks, blue and grey boxes in stores and restaurants, or ask for facilities at attractions. [2]

Being a Green Tourist

Being a green tourist is really about living a greener, healthier life anywhere. It's about each day trying to find ways to have a little less impact and give a little more back to the planet and ourselves (including joy and pleasure, of course). So, as an exercise, we broke a typical trip and a typical day down into manageable chunks: how you prepare, how you get around, how you buy things, how you have fun, how you do business ... and we came up with a checklist that probably someone as tireless as Mother Theresa or Ghandi couldn't get through completely even if they had this guide.

Nevertheless, we've included a somewhat abridged edition meant as a sort of menu that you can select a few things from each day. Don't try to do it all at once — perfection is the enemy of the good.

Top Ten Ways to do Green Tourism:

1. Think and Dream Green: Read Up and Get Excited.
2. Pack for a Green Adventure.
3. Go Green: Choose Sustainable Transportation.
4. Stay Green: Choose Green Accommodations.
5. Eat and Drink: Locally and, if Possible, Organically.
6. Reduce, Reuse, and Recycle.
7. Shop Green, Spend Green, and Do Green Business.
8. Indulge in Green and Healthy Things:
9. Share the Wealth
10. Move and Shake

1. Think and Dream Green: Read Up and Get Excited

It's always good to start by feeding your mind and soul. What ideas come to mind when you think about green cities, and exploring cities in a green way? This guidebook is a start, but there's so much more on the net and in print that covers environment, eco-tourism, and cities.

Start with the Green Tourism Association web site at www. greentourism.on.ca. It offers info and tips on green tourism, as well as an extensive virtual eco-tourism resource centre that connects you to eco-tourism sources and resources from all over the world.

For more Toronto-centric on-line information, visit the City of Toronto site www.city.toronto.on.ca, and start with the Environmental Task Force page. It has some pretty comprehensive directories of local groups and projects as well as City initiatives. Most Green Tourism Association members (see page 155) have web sites, as do many of the listed Resource Groups (see page 151).

If you prefer the printed page, pick up or order any of the following books exploring "other" aspects of Toronto:

- *Secret Toronto* by Scott Mitchell
- *Mini Rough Guide Toronto* by Phil Lee and Helen Lovekin
- *Hip Guide to Toronto* by K. von Hahn
- *I Remember Sunnyside* and *Toronto Sketches* by Mike Filey
- *Lobster's Kids' Guide to Exploring Toronto* by N. Comeau
- *Toronto the Wild: Field Notes of an Urban Naturalist* by Wayne Grady
- *Accidental City: Transformation of Toronto* by Robert Fulford (for urban history buffs)
- *The Shape of The City: Toronto Struggles with Modern Planning* by Jane Jacobs and John Sewell (for urban politics buffs)
- *Special Places: The Changing Ecosystems of the Toronto Region* edited by Betty Roots, Donald Chant and Conrad Heidenreich

Once you get to Toronto, you can also find other useful guidebooks and maps at Open Air Maps and Books (25 Toronto St., 363-0719). Visit any local book store for books on Toronto. Or drop in to any public library and see what you can find. If they don't have what you want — ask for it and they may order something specially for you.

2. Pack for a Green Adventure

Be prepared — it's not a bad motto when it comes to green tourism, because things you take for granted at home are not always in your suitcase or available right next door to your Bed & Breakfast. Packing light but smart is a great way to help make green decisions easier. Of course you can decide how fanatical you want to get, but here's a start for a what-to-pack checklist:

- Your research material (green things to do, people to see, places to go).
- A mug, a plate, and some cutlery (or one of those groovy multipurpose implements) for an impromptu picnic or for some delicious food in the privacy of your room.
- A bungee cord is so versatile — it will secure stuff on your bike but can also double as a clothes line.
- Drawing pencils and your favourite paper (recording your trip this way can be more fun and less toxic than taking photographs).
- Rechargeable batteries and a recharger (if you are bringing anything electronic).
- A small portable musical instrument — making your own music requires no non-renewable resources.
- A string or cloth bag that you can use if you buy more local art and products than you can carry freehand.
- If you're REALLY going for it, a plastic bag to store your apple cores until you find the nearest composter. (See page 12 for info on composting.)
- A cloth napkin and/or handkerchief to cut down on paper use.
- A fountain pen (it's reusable).
- A roll up yoga or exercise mat if you have a regular routine at home, so that you can keep energized and centred while you're in Toronto.
- Inspirational reading — ecological poetry and prose.
- Clothes:
  - that are easy to clean and dry in your hotel room — elegant but easy care
  - that you can get down and dirty in — for cycling, walking, planting a tree
  - good comfortable walking shoes

Lake Ontario is the only source of Toronto's drinking water. [3]

3. Go Green: Choose Sustainable Transportation

Transporting yourself around Toronto can be a moving experience. There are so many pleasant and convenient sustainable transportation options to choose from, it isn't too challenging to go green, even with minimal planning.

Toronto has one of the better transit systems on the continent, and in 1995 was named by *Bicycling* magazine as the best city for cycling in North America. Its compact, pre-automobile downtown also makes it a very walkable city. See the Getting Around section that starts on page 26 for more practical information.

Detailing all the reasons for choosing sustainable transportation in this guide would kill far too many trees. But in a nutshell, automobile and truck transportation is not only the largest source of greenhouse gases in Canada, it also contributes in a big way to frustrating and costly traffic congestion, smog (which causes 1,000 deaths in Toronto each year), noise, injury and death caused by accidents, social inequity, and destruction of valuable farm land.

See the Centre for Sustainable Transportation website at www.cstctd.org for information on the impacts of transportation. Or check out the **Moving the Economy** website at www.city.toronto.on.ca/mte for sustainable transportation success stories. You can find the City of Toronto Environmental Task Force website at www.city.toronto.on.ca/council/environtf_index.htm for a great directory of transportation projects, groups and initiatives in the Toronto region.

Meanwhile, here's a hierarchy of transportation options that you can apply while you're in Toronto or anywhere to help you move more lightly on the earth:

- Walk, stroll, saunter, or skip — feet are the most sustainable mode of transportation and can be one of the most pleasant, especially in a city designed for them.
- Cycle or in-line skate. It's healthy, fun, and one of the fastest modes of transportation in the congested downtown core. (See the Getting Around section, page 26 for info on bike rental and programs for safety and promotion.)
- Take transit. It's so easy, fast and affordable in Toronto, and it can be a great way of experiencing local culture.
- If you can, arrive by train or bus. Trains are romantic and pleasant and both trains and buses get you right into downtown and avoid the hassle of getting in from the airport. Not only that, air travel is even worse than

driving in terms of environmental impact. One transatlantic flight has the same effect as two years of an average person's car travel. When you're coming from across the ocean, this is difficult to avoid, but it's good to keep in mind if you do have other options.

- Every once in a while, at the end of a long weary day of walking or cycling, have a human powered pedicab / rickshaw or a natural gas taxi whisk you home.
- If you must arrive by car, park it when you get here and don't pick it up until the end of your trip. Driving in Toronto can be an expensive, frustrating hassle. See if you can share the trip or do a drive-away. If you are renting a car, try to choose an alternative fuel vehicle, or a fuel efficient one. Car sharing is a new option in some communities (see **Autoshare** in the Resource Groups section) so take advantage of that option if you live in Toronto or are not too far away.
- In general, try to use the most sustainable transportation option available for the purpose. Combine modes or eliminate trips altogether, where you can.

If you are interested in delving deeper, a very rich sustainable transportation community exists in Toronto, including a Bicycle Choir (yes — they sing and ride at the same time — watch for them passing by on the street, or pick up their first CD at the Urbane Cyclist). If you sing and cycle, you're welcome to join in on one of their Monday night rehearsals. Call Song Cycles at 338-5088. You can also join in on the Critical Mass ride on the last Friday of every month at 6 pm at the corner of Yonge and Temperance Street. At Critical Mass, hundreds of cyclists take to the streets for a lively rush hour ride.

4. Stay Green: Choose Green Accommodations

These days, more and more hotels make it much easier to be green. (see the Accommodations section, page 24). These environmentally-friendly hotels may provide recycling, composting, optional laundry and chemical-free dry-cleaning, energy efficient heat and light, low flow toilets, organic and veggie food, progressive employee programs and more… It's great if you can stay at a hotel like this. If not, you can still make a difference by making sure the lights are off when you leave the room, and by finding and using a nearby recycling or composting bin. (see page 12 for info on recycling and composting).

If you are staying with friends and family, your exciting green adventure may be intriguing to them.

We've found that other people seeing you have fun works much better than preaching. Inviting them out to a delicious organic meal or buying them a locally made green gift can be quite persuasive.

If it seems appropriate, ask the hotel establishment gently if they have any of these green options or if they plan to in the future. Gentle prodding over time by enough visitors can do wonders to create a demand for greener options. After all, the customer is always right.

5. Eat and Drink: Locally and, If Possible, Organically

It's tough, but somebody's got to do it. If you make it your goal to sample all the local specialities and veggie and organic delights available in Toronto you'll have your work cut out for you. For more details, see the Cuisine section and highlights in each area in this Guide. You should also be sure to pick up your free copy of the *Vegetarian Guide to Toronto* available in most health food stores and healthy restaurants.

To complement the delicious food, ask to sample one of Toronto's local brews. Amsterdam, Steam Whistle, Upper Canada and Granite are just a few of our hometown ales, nutbrowns and lagers.

Beyond pure pleasure and personal health, there are so many reasons to eat local, healthy, and if possible, organic food. Pesticides are more than unhealthy for our bodies and for our farmland. And pests are becoming increasingly resistant to pesticides, forcing farmers to up the ante and use even more.

Eating locally grown and produced food has all sorts of advantages. Not only does it support local farmers, it also means that the food has less distance to travel. It gets to your table fresher, and it won't have logged so many polluting kilometres in a truck. For more information, see the Canadian Organic Growers website at www.cog.ca/ and the Foodshare Metro Toronto website at www.toronto.com/E/V/TORON/0020/14/03/.

6. Reduce, Reuse, and Recycle

You can apply the good old three R's to tourism in the traditional sense, or you can be a little more creative.

REDUCE: Reduce your ecological footprint. The Ecological Footprint is a tool used to measure human impact on nature. It measures the productive land and water we occupy to produce all the resources we consume and then to take in all the waste we create.

Find out about Toronto's Ecological Footprint on the web at www.city.toronto.on.ca/energy/footprint.htm. Calculate your footprint at www.mec.ca/coop/communit/meccomm/ecofoot.htm.

Complete a more comprehensive survey at www.city .toronto.on.ca/energy/quest.htm.

Toronto is reducing its energy use. Check the City of Toronto Environmental Task Force site for information on the off-the-grid Healthy House, Deep Lake Water Cooling, the Better Buildings Partnership, and Toronto's first working windmill.

Reduce your energy use. Turn off lights, and use appliances sparingly.

Reduce toxic waste: Take your clothes to a chemical-free dry-cleaner (you can find them in the Yellow Pages), or rent a digital (chemical-free) camera or video-camera from Vistek (496 Queen E. 365-1777) or M&A Photovideo (432 Queen E. 362-6902) and email your photos to your friends and family.

Travel less. Explore one area in depth. If you live in Toronto, take a vacation to get to know your own city. It's surprising how much you don't get to explore about your own city when you're all caught up in the challenges of day-to-day life.

Do less — Just hang out and walk around, take in the sights and the local culture. Go to a park and stare into space. Contemplate Toronto's clouds.

Buy less. Save your money for pleasure: buying local art, organic food, environmental products, getting a massage or supporting a local cause.

The Toronto Public Library (TPL) system provides free access to books and other reading materials as well as free internet access and other community services. Visitors are welcome to use the system but can't borrow materials. Call the TPL's answerline at 393-7668 for more info.

REUSE: Toronto is the land of re-used opportunity. Check the Toronto Environmental Alliance's Use-It Re-Use It Guide (Call TEA for information on how to get the latest edition at 596-0660). Meanwhile, here are a few ideas for starters:

Fashion: For funky vintage wear, check out Goodwill, Value Village, Salvation Army or Ex-Toggery stores (there are numerous locations in the phone book — head for the one nearest you). Or try the vintage clothing stores in and around Kensington Market and Queen St., west of University Avenue.

Re-use books and magazines. Harbord just west of Spadina and Queen W. from Spadina to just past Bathurst are great places to find used bookstores. Find a used CD shop and buy a local independent band's CD. Buy funky art fom a gallery on Queen W. Pick up some cool vintage jewellery from a store in Kensington Market. Find a nice used camera (or just about anything else) at a pawnshop around Queen E. and Church Street.

Re-use your shoes. Don't buy new ones, get your old ones repaired at one of the many shoe repair stores across the city. Check www.toronto.com "shoe repair" for various listings.

For furniture (if you have a berth in your train or a really big pannier on your bike) — check out Toronto's many antique and used furniture shops. Also try places that sell furniture and home supplies that they've rescued from demolition before renovation. Call Habitat for Humanity's "ReStore" for info (755-7353).

Need some equipment? Try a Rent-All. Check the Yellow Pages.

RECYCLE: You can recycle your cans, glass bottles, and newspapers using the rectangular silver 3-slotted bins on sidewalks. Recyling is also available in most Toronto buildings and recreational and entertainment areas. Blue boxes are for cans, glass and plastic, grey boxes are for newsprint and cardboard. If you forgot to bring rechargeable batteries, ask about the toxic taxi if your hotel can't deal with toxic waste. Call 392-4546 for more info on waste reduction.

Compost. There are more and more opportunities to publicly compost, vermi- and otherwise. You should be able to spot one before the bag of orange peels from your picnic starts to turn. Call 392-4689 for info on composting and for compost demo sites.

If you've finished with your book, donate it to a charitable organization like Goodwill for resale and reuse. They also accept clothes, accessories and other reuseable goods, so you know what to do if you've bought so many local products that you have to free up some space in your suitcase.

7. Shop Green, Spend Green, and Do Green Business

The way you spend your money can make a huge difference to Toronto folks and the planet at the same time.

SHOPPING GREEN AND LOCALLY: When you buy local products from local establishments, you're boosting Toronto's economy. You have also reduced the distance the product had to travel by almost 100%. The extra bonus for you is that you'll end up with something nobody has back home.

For local fashion, food, books and arts and crafts, poke along key areas: Queen west of Bathurst, Kensington Market (food and clothes with cafés thrown in), the Beaches, and more (see the neighbourhood "Things To Do, See, Buy & Eat" sections). Bring your own bag if possible.

Great local bookshops include: This Ain't the Rosedale Library on Church St., Pages on Queen and Book City at various locations.

It's especially good to patronize local businesses that show a concern for the environment. It helps to create a demand for green products and practices. See the Green Tourism Association members list in the back of this guide (page 155).

To buy strictly green products, check out **Grassroots Environmental Products** (see Member Listings page 167) — they have everything from eco laundry soap to plants and paper and solar radios.

There are also a few special one-of-a-kind local events where you can get local and green gifts. You may end up being in Toronto at the right time for things like the Toronto Environmental Alliance green gift sale, the One of a Kind Craft Show and Sale (Spring and Fall) the Spring Herb Fair, and more. See page 36 for up-to-date information sources.

SPENDING GREEN: To keep money circulating locally, Toronto, like many cities, has a Local Exchange Trading System (978-0536). The St. Lawrence Market area also has a community currency called the "Toronto Dollar". It encourages people and businesses within the community to use and promote other area groups and businesses and foster collective social and economic benefits. Visit www.toronto.com for info.

If you need to change your money, why not try one of the many branches of the local Metro Credit Union. Check the phone book for the location nearest you.

DOING GREEN BUSINESS: If you're mixing business and green tourism pleasure, there are some good options for making the business part more efficient. Most downtown hotels offer business travellers meeting facilities, fully-serviced work centres and computer hook-ups in rooms. Alternatively, try one of Toronto's many Internet cafés, or even the public libraries, which offer a quiet space and a free Internet connection. (See page 11.)

Furnished office space is available throughout the city — most providers offer flexible leases and fully-serviced offices. Check the Yellow Pages under "office rentals" for listings.

If you're attending or organizing a conference or convention, ask about the availability of environmental services and programs at the convention facility.

8. Indulge in Green and Healthy Things

Even (and especially) if you're having lots of fun, you can still tread lightly and do good things for the city and the planet. Here are just a few win-win options:

COMMUNE WITH NATURE: There's so much more of it in the City than you would first imagine — both flora and fauna. While you're there, imagine what we'd do without it. Check our listings for parks and green spaces in each area.

TAKE IN THE ARTS: Arts touch the soul, challenging, inspiring, and replenishing us. Much contemporary art is based on ecological and social themes. This and other art thrives in Toronto. Check area listings and Arts magazines (see page 40) for details.

Alternative theatre listings can be found on the Toronto Theatre Alliance website, www.culturenet.ca/tta. Toronto is also a film capital of the world. Check the Festivals and Events section (see page 36). You can find more information on page 36 for a variety of film festivals, including an environmental film festival, and page 41 for repertory cinemas. Music-wise, there's just about anything you could want. Check the weeklies. (See page 18.)

GET PHYSICAL: Whether it's to push your limits or centre yourself or just get your blood circulating, there are so many options:

Why not be an urban voyageur? Rent a canoe or kayak at **Mountain Equipment Co-op** or Trailhead downtown and head for a river. Or if you're here in the spring, join the **Toronto Region Conservation Authority** and the

Wilderness Canoe Association in the "Paddle the Don" event, a chance for people to canoe down the Don River from Eglinton to Lake Ontario. Call 661-6600 ext. 5397 for info.

Don't mind heights? Climb a mountain at one of many rock climbing facilities in Toronto. Try Joe Rockhead's Climbing Gym at 29 Fraser Ave., 538-7670. It's Canada's first indoor rock climbing facility and it also offers equipment rental.

Yoga and other such classes are available all over the city. Check for ads in *Vitality Magazine*. Pick them up at the local health food store.

On a hot, muggy summer day, cool off at one of the many public indoor or outdoor pools around town. See www.city.toronto.on.ca/parks for pool locations.

Who needs a Stairmaster? Just visit the CN Tower and climb 1,776 stairs up the world's tallest building at this annual charity event. See www.stairclimb.org for info.

WINTER FUN: Ice-skating is a great way to spend a nice, sunny afternoon, or a cool, crisp evening. The rink in front of City Hall and the rock-encircled rink at Ryerson University are especially romantic. Visit www.city.toronto.on.ca/parks for other rink and arena locations.

Hit the slopes. Snowboarding and skiing are within the city limits at Centennial Park in the west end and Earle Bales Park in the north. Equipment rentals are available there. You can also rent skis from **Mountain Equipment Co-op** and Trailhead downtown. (See pages 50, 52.)

Head for the hills. Grab a toboggan and take a ride down one of many hills in the city. Some of the best are located in Riverdale Park, High Park and Centennial Park.

GET TO KNOW LOCAL CULTURE: Toronto is a diverse and multicultural city. Get involved in cultural events, language classes, or just hang out in one neighbourhood long enough to really get to know how Toronto folks and their different neighbourhoods tick.

GREEN LOVIN': Visit Come As You Are (701 Queen W., 504-7934), Good for Her (175 Harbord, 588-0900) and Seduction (577 Yonge, 966-6969) for progressive sexual products and information. Priape (465 Church, 586-9914) serves the gay community.

PRACTICE NATURAL HEALTH: If you get sick or if you

are the more preventative type and you just want to stay healthy, here are a few sources of outlets for natural health products and where to find more. Check internet for listings of local health stores supplying natural vitamins, supplements and herbal medicines at www.toronto.com. And make sure to pick up a free copy of *Vitality Magazine*, they cover a broad range of natural health issues, events, and options. In particular, check out Hoopers Pharmacy (24 Wellesley W., 928-3366), Thuna (298 Danforth 465-3366), Noah's (322 Bloor W. 968-7930) and Thompson's (844 Yonge, 922-2300).

And after a long day of green tourism, why not indulge in a relaxing massage of just about any variety. Check *Vitality Magazine* or the yellow pages for ads.

9. Share the Wealth

Don't keep urban green tourism to yourself. Share it:
WITH YOUR KIDS — THE NEXT GENERATION: If you're in Toronto with children there are all sorts of ways to inspire future generations of green tourism practitioners. You might want to take in canoe and kayak lessons at Harbourfront; visit the beautiful Children's Garden in High Park; explore science and technology at the **Ontario Science Centre**, and more. For one of the best sources of ideas on what you can do with kids in Toronto, look for *Lobster's Kids Guide to Toronto* by Natalie Ann Comeau at your nearest bookstore or online.

If you and your kids both need a "time out" try Scadding Court Community Centre. It offers temporary or emergency childcare between 8:30 and 4. Call 392-0335 ext. 235 for info. Some attractions also offer childcare and have daycare facilities or children's rooms on site. Contact the attraction to confirm.
WITH YOUR FRIENDS, FAMILY, AND COLLEAGUES: In Toronto or back home, invite friends to enjoy green tourism with you.

10. Move and Shake

If, after doing green tourism for a while, you feel inspired to go one step further, why not get involved in helping to green Toronto or to promote green tourism in your own city? While you're in Toronto, spend an afternoon planting trees, hook up with the Critical Mass ride, join the Bike choir for an evening, or volunteer for a day with a local community or environmental group. You can find more information in the Members Listings and Resources at the back of this Guide, and in extensive directories on the Environmental Task Force website.

When you get home, talk to friends and local movers and shakers about getting green tourism going there. The Green Tourism Association is working on a start-up kit for other cities, and we're always glad to share our Toronto experience in getting things going.

Key Information and Resources

Planning Your Trip: Key Sources

Before you arrive or while you're here, the following resources offer up to date info:

TOURISM TORONTO (Queen's Quay Terminal-Harbourfront, 207 Queens Quay W., Suite 590. 203-2500 or toll-free 1-800-499-2514, www.torontotourism.com). Kiosk at City Hall: M-Sat. in summer.

ACCESS TORONTO (338-0338, TTY: 338-0889, www.city.toronto.on.ca/ services/accesstoronto.htm). Access Toronto is the public information service for the City of Toronto. Open M–F 8 to 5. It provides a wide variety of services to help you get information about Toronto's municipal government.

ONTARIO TRAVEL INFORMATION CENTRE (220 Yonge Toronto Eaton Centre, 1-800-668-2746, www.ontariotravel.net). General information for travel in Ontario including trip planning, travel councillors, special events, canoe routes, and park entrance fees, entry regulations to Ontario, currency, road reports and reservations.

INFO T.O. (Metro Toronto Convention Centre, 255 Front W. 585-8000). Filled with information on the city's attractions, events and nightlife, INFO T.O. offers visitors and residents an ideal stop for information, reservations and ticket purchases. Open daily May–Sept. 8–8, Oct.–Apr. 8–5. For more info, contact Toronto Tours at 869-1372.

TRAVELLERS' AID SOCIETY

- Toronto Coach Terminal (610 Bay St., 596-8647).
- Union Station (65 Front W., 366-7788).
- Pearson International Airport Terminal 1, 2, and 3 (905-676-2868).

Provides info as well as free accommodation reservation service and other help in crisis situations.

Helpful Daily and Weekly Information

NOW MAGAZINE. Available free at newspaper boxes, many restaurants and cafés. Probably the best source of music, theatre and arts listings you'll find — and it's everywhere.(www.nowtoronto.com).

EYE MAGAZINE. Also a great free source of weekly listings and available at newspaper boxes, many

restaurants and cafés everywhere. (www.eye.net).
WHERE TORONTO. Monthly magazine offering tour, accommodation and attraction information. Found at many hotels and attractions
TORONTO.COM. Provides on-line information about just about anything in Toronto. (www.toronto.com).
TORONTO LIFE MAGAZINE. Monthly magazine featuring profiles, articles, and listings on Toronto events. (www.torontolife.com).
TORONTO STAR. Every Thursday there is a special section: What's On. (www.thestar.com).
Also check subway stations and street corner boxes for free daily newspapers with lots of event info and listings.

Practicalities

Weather

Toronto's a great destination any time of year, you just have to be properly dressed for it. In a perfect summer (June through August), daytime highs will be in the mid-20s C (70s F) and evenings will hover around 15°C (60°F). But it can get hot, humid and sticky, sometimes as high 40°C (100°F). Winters (November to March) are cold, sometimes damp, and are blessed with snow (slush if temperatures rise a bit). Look for 0°C (32°F) averages by day and below freezing nights around -7°C (18°F), with occasional extreme lows and biting wind chill factors. During spring (April and May) and fall (September and October), temperatures will move around mid-range. For full up to date weather details, see The Weather Network at www.theweathernetwork.com.

Time Zone

Toronto sits in the Eastern Standard Time Zone.

Notable Holidays

On holidays, all government offices and services, credit institutions and large corporations are closed, as are many small businesses. Most restaurants, hotels and tourist-related businesses remain open on holidays.
JANUARY. New Year's Day (Jan. 1st).
APRIL. Good Friday, Easter Sunday, Easter Monday (Government offices closed; corporations usually close on one of the two days).
MAY. Victoria Day (Monday after 3rd Sunday).
JUNE. School summer holidays (end of June to early

September) mean more crowds and prices are generally higher.
JULY. Canada Day (July 1st).
AUGUST. Simcoe Day (1st Monday).
SEPTEMBER. Labour Day (1st Monday).
OCTOBER. Thanksgiving Day (1st or 2nd Monday).
NOVEMBER. Remembrance Day (Nov. 11th — credit institutions and government only).
DECEMBER. Christmas Day (Dec. 25th), Boxing Day (Dec. 26th).

Banking & Money

CURRENCY: The Canadian Dollar is made up of 100 cents. Bills come in 5, 10, 20, 50, 100 and 1000-dollar denominations. Some stores and gas stations will not accept $50 or $100 bills after dark. Coins come in $2 (toonie), $1 (loonie), 25 cents (quarter), 10 cents (dime), 5 cents (nickel), 1 cent (penny).
BANKS: Major branches are open Monday to Friday usually from 10 am – 4 pm, with extended hours on Fridays. Automated Banking Machines (ABMs or ATMs) are plentiful. Many are located in shopping centres, convenience & grocery stores and along downtown streets.
CHANGING MONEY: Currency can be converted at all major banks and foreign exchange service agencies. Along Yonge, King and Queen Sts. there are money changers open regularly. Some agencies include:

- Money Mart, (920-4146), open 24 hours.
- Thomas Cook Foreign Exchange. (304-6130).
- Custom House Currency Exchange. (214-6002).
- Foreign Currency Exchange. (346-6884).

Each have various locations around the city. Ask at your accommodation reception or info cenre for more info.
CREDIT CARDS & TRAVELLERS CHEQUES: For lost or stolen cards, call:

- American Express. (1-800-869-3016).
- AMEX Travellers Cheques. (1-800-807-6234).
- Mastercard Global Service Centre. (1-800-247-4623).
- VISA Assistance Centre. (1-800-847-2911).
- VISA Travellers Cheques. (1-800-227-6811).

Tax & Tipping

SALES TAX: Two sales taxes in Ontario tally up to 15% - the 7% Federal Goods and Services Tax (GST) and the 8% Provincial Sales Tax (PST). These are usually added on top of the listed price at the cash register. Tourists and non-residents may be eligible to claim a tax refund on goods purchased in Canada and being taken out of the country. Separate forms for each tax must be filled out at customs/border crossings. For locations of GST and PST refund forms and more information phone toll free: GST 1-800-668-4748, PST 1-800-668-5810.

TIPPING: Tip 10% to 15% in restaurants, bars and clubs, or for taxi drivers, delivery persons, and hairdressers /barbers. You are free to withhold or reduce the tip if you feel the service wasn't good. (Note: the GST and PST taxes equal 15% — to find out a 15% tip just add the two taxes).

Communication

Local calls by pay telephones are $0.25 within the (416) and most (905) area codes. Loonies ($1), quarters ($0.25), dimes ($0.10), and nickels ($0.05) are accepted. Most payphones accept credit cards. Toronto has a number of pay phone service providers. Some do not provide change and calling cards/quick change cards are not always accepted. Cards can be purchased at most convenience stores throughout the city. See individual pay phones for instructions and rates.

All telephone numbers listed in this guide are (416) area codes unless otherwise noted. Beginning in **March 2001**, all local calls within the City of Toronto will require a 10-digit phone number that includes either the **416** area code or the new **647** area code.

INTERNET: Ask if the place you're staying offers Internet services. Most public libraries also offer access to the internet and Internet cafés have become increasingly common. See www.toronto.com or the local yellow pages for listings.

Cuisine / Dining Out

There are over 7,000 restaurants in Toronto. Within each section of this guide, a few of our top picks are mentioned. We hope you will also check out these great resources:

TORONTO VEGETARIAN ASSOCIATION (544-9800). Info on a large number of vegetarian restaurants with diverse cuisine at many price ranges and all over the city.

NOW'S CITY GUIDE TO TORONTO. The Urban Adventurer's Ultimate Field Guide is available in local bookstores. Most public places and many restaurants listed are smoke-free establishments; call ahead to confirm.

For a listing of smoke free establishments check www.city.toronto.on.ca/health/smokefree.

Wine, Beer & Spirits

The provincial government's Liquor Control Board of Ontario (LCBO) monitors the sale of alcohol. Liquor or beer is not available at supermarkets or convenience stores. Liquor can be purchased at LCBO stores, and beer can be purchased at the Beer Store. There are many convenient locations throughout the city. It is illegal to drink alcohol outside of licensed establishments or private homes including parks and any outdoor locations not licensed by the LCBO. You must be 19+ years of age to purchase and consume alcohol legally. It's a good idea to bring photo identification with you if you plan on having a drink.

Public Washrooms

Washrooms are available in all restaurants, bars, or clubs (they prefer paying customers), service stations and civic centres. Some public buildings allow access to their facilities, and some parks have washrooms open on a seasonal basis.

Specialized Information

Street Sense

Toronto is known for being clean and safe. But it never hurts to be careful after dark and to think about the same things here as you would in your home town. Use common sense. There are homeless people, window washers (called squeegee kids) and beggars in Toronto. Most are harmless and many are friendly.

Information for Women

Toronto is a fantastic place for the female explorer, safe, friendly and fun, but do consider the following when travelling alone:

- Try to arrive at your destination before dark. TTC offers a special 'Request Stop' service for women (see green tip on next page).
- When checking into an accommodation, look at the room first and make sure doors and windows are secure.
- In the quieter areas, avoid wandering alone at night and take caution just as you would at home.

HELPFUL RESOURCES:

- U of T Women's Centre (568 Spadina, 978-8201).
- Toronto Women's Bookstore (73 Harbord, 922-8744). Books by and about women, is also a community resource centre.

- Women's Counselling, Referral and Education centre (525 Bloor W., 534-7501).
- www.journeywoman.com an online travel resource to inspire women everywhere to travel well and to travel safely.

Request Stop: The REQUEST STOP program is available to women travelling by TTC bus between 9 pm and 5 am. Through this service, women are allowed to get off the bus between regular TTC stops. Please make your request at least one stop ahead of the desired location. The driver must be able to stop safely.

Gay Toronto

Toronto is blessed with one of the largest gay communities in North America (see Church-Wellesley Village page 84). Our first gay pride celebration was held in 1971 and has now grown to over 700,000 people at the annual parade in June. Look for the rainbow decal at stores and accommodations. Here are some helpful resources:

XTRA MAGAZINE (925-XTRA). A bi-weekly free newspaper.
T.A.G.L.A.R.C. (964-6600). Info on gay services & counselling in Toronto.
www.gaycanada.com. Canadian Gay internet resource centre.
www.clga.ca/archives. Canadian Lesbian and Gay Archives website focusing mainly on gay rights and advocacy.
GLAD DAY BOOKSHOP (598A Yonge, 961-4161). Specializes in gay, lesbian, bisexual, transgender literature.

Accessibility

Most cities could stand to be more accessible and friendly to people with physical disabilities. Toronto is no exception. However in recent years, savvy movers and shakers have succeeded in sensitizing planners, designers, transport operators and businesses to people with special needs, with the result that an urban green tourism experience is much more pleasant and possible than it used to be. The member listings at the back of this Guide indicate accessible sites with a ♿. Here are some helpful resources:

CENTRE FOR INDEPENDENT LIVING (599-2458). Information and referrals for individuals with disabilities.
HEARING IMPAIRED SOCIETY (1-800-665-0354).
TOBIAS HOUSE (690-3185). Provides attendant care and equipment rentals for short or long-term visitors. Call two weeks ahead for availability.

TTY (ACCESS TORONTO) (338-0889). Teletypewriter for the hearing impaired.
WHEELTRANS (393-4222). A special transit service for people who travel in a wheelchair and cannot ride on conventional public transit vehicles. Call a day in advance of your visit to get a two-week pass. Visitors to Toronto must register with Wheel-Trans to obtain a temporary passenger number to use the service. The service is the same price as a regular TTC fare and available every day between 6:30 am and 1 am. An escort may ride with you.

Worship

Toronto welcomes and is home to people of all religious backgrounds — far too many to list here. To find places of worship, check the Yellow Pages under religious organizations. You can also pick up *Vitality Magazine* at local Health shops. Or scan the postings at Trinity St. Paul Church (427 Bloor St. W., 922-4954) for other spiritual communities.

Accommodations

Toronto is full of hotels and other accommodations but some are making an effort to be green or to support green efforts, or both. We've listed the ones we know about. Accommodation in Toronto is like most big cities — dorms and hostels are usually under $30 but hotels can range up to $300 per night. Call **Tourism Toronto** for reservations and prices. (See page 18).

Accommodation Sources

BED & BREAKFAST ASSOCIATION OF DOWNTOWN TORONTO (410-3938, www.bnbinfo.com).
TRAVELLERS AID SOCIETY Free accommodation reservation service. (See page 18.)
TOURISM TORONTO Free hotel reservation service. (See page 18.)

Downtown Hotels

BOND PLACE HOTEL (65 Dundas E., 362-6061).
DELTA CHELSEA HOTEL (33 Gerrard W., 595-1975, www.deltachelsea.com).
HOTEL INTERCONTINENTAL (220 Bloor W., 960-5200).
ROYAL YORK HOTEL (100 Front W., 368-2511).
SHERATON CENTRE TORONTO HOTEL (123 Queen W., 361-1000).

THE SUTTON PLACE HOTEL (955 Bay St., 924-9221).
TOWN INN SUITES (620 Church, 964 -3311, www.towninn.com).

Downtown Bed & Breakfasts

BEACONSFIELD B&B (38 Beaconsfield, 535-3338, beacon@idirect.com).
LES AMIS VEGETARIAN BED AND BREAKFAST (31 Granby St., 591-0635, les-amis@bbtoronto.com).
TORONTO BED & BREAKFAST (Box 269, 253 College St., 588-8800, beds@torontobandb.com).

Downtown Hostels

GLOBAL VILLAGE BACKPACKERS (460 King St. W., 703-8540, www.globalbackpackers.com).
CANADIANA INTERNATIONAL GUESTHOUSE (40 & 42 Widmer St., 598-9090, canadiana@inforamp.net).
HAVINN INTERNATIONAL 118 Spadina Rd., 922-5220, home.echo-on.net/~havinn/).
HOSTELLING INTERNATIONAL (76 Church St., 971-4440, www.hostellingint-gl.on.ca).
NEILL-WYCIK COLLEGE HOSTEL (96 Gerrard St. E., 977-2320 or toll-free 1-800-268-4358, www.inforamp.net ~wycik). Summer only.
TORONTO BUDGET HOSTEL (223 Church St., 703-3939).

Downtown Dorms/University Rooms

RYERSON POLYTECHNIC UNIVERSITY CONFERENCE SERVICES (160 Mutual St., Suite 101, 979-5296, www.ryerson.ca). May to August.

Outside Downtown

MARIGOLD INTERNATIONAL TRAVELLERS HOSTEL (2011 Dundas St. W., 536-8824).
MIMICO HOSTEL AND BED & BREAKFAST (150 Queens, 251-6208, http://home.ican.net/~derekb/).
THE GUILD INN (201 Guildwood Parkway, Scarborough, 261-3331).

Camping

GLEN ROUGE CAMPGROUND (Kingston Rd., just east of Sheppard, 392-8186, parks@metrodesk. metrotoronto.on.ca).
INDIAN LINE CAMPGROUND (7625 Finch W., 905-678-1233 or toll free 1-800-304-9728).

Going Greener — Getting Around

Toronto offers a whole range of well connected and sustainable transportation options (see page 8). It is also a well-organized city, laid out in a grid system. Major streets run pretty much north/south and east/west. In fact, if you can orient yourself to the landmark CN Tower downtown, you will always stay on track. Lake Ontario borders Toronto on the south. The CN Tower is right by the lake and in the centre of downtown. The Hudson Bay tower marks Bloor and Yonge.

Toronto is a great city for walking — especially downtown. But it is a big city, so bikes or in-line skates are also a good option. Or in the summer, hail a rickshaw to take you through downtown. Public transit (Toronto Transit Commission — TTC and GO Transit) will get you anywhere locally or regionally. The plentiful taxis are also a good option. If you must drive, try to car pool or share, and be sure you bone up on our Highway Traffic Act and our local bylaws. Cars have to stop for people crossing at crosswalks and exiting streetcars, and they also have to stay out of designated bike lanes. Traffic can be terrible, slow and frustrating during the weekday morning and evening rush hours.

The poem in the front of this guide was written for the Toronto Transit Commission's "Poetry On The Way", which presents Canadian poetry to TTC riders on placards in Toronto's buses, streetcars, and subways. Poetry On The Way is a passenger-run program, supported by the Canada Council. [4]

Bike Routes and Trails

Toronto bike routes and trails form an almost unbroken network around town, and many are through publicly-owned green spaces. Most Toronto bike routes and trails are accessible by TTC. You can take your bicycle on buses, streetcars or on the subway seven days a week anytime except during rush hours (M–F 6:30–9:30 am and 3:30–6:30 pm at the drivers' discretion). There is also bike parking at most subway stations.

CITY OF TORONTO CYCLING SOURCES:

TORONTO CYCLING COMMITTEE (392-7592, www.city. toronto.on.ca/cycling). Great bike map of the city. Watch for Toronto's Cycling Ambassadors who offer lots of great bicycling information. You'll see them at many events around the city.

PRINT RESOURCES:

The Great Toronto Bicycling Guide by Elliott Katz.
Practical Pedalling by Sarah Hood (available through www.detourpublications.com). A local cycling guide book.

Bike & Blade Rentals

Why not rent a bike for the day or for your entire stay? It's a great way to explore both city streets and green spaces. Most bike rentals require a major credit card and a deposit. Some of the following locations may also rent in-line skates. Call ahead.

BATHURST CYCLE (913 Bathurst, 533-7510).
BROWN'S SPORTS & CYCLE (2447 Bloor W., 763-4176).
CYCLEMANIA (113 Danforth, 466-0330).
CYCLE PATH (1510 Danforth, 463-5346).
CYCLE PATH (2106 Yonge, 487-1717).
EUROPE BOUND (49 Front E., 601-0854).
HIGH PARK CYCLE AND SPORTS (24 Ronson, 614-6689).
MCBRIDE'S CYCLES (2923 Dundas. W., 763-5652).
RECYCLE BIKE COMPANY (SET ME FREE) (2130 Queen E., 698-3756).
RECYCLE BIKE COMPANY (SET ME FREE) (381 Roncesvalles, 532-4147).
STREETCITY BIKES (1178 Queen E., 466-7492).
SPOKES AND SPORTS (1889 Avenue, 787-6238).
WHEEL EXCITEMENT (5 Rees, 260-9000).

Approximately 1,465,000 passengers use the TTC every day. Imagine if those were car trips. [5]

Public Transit

TORONTO TRANSIT SYSTEM (TTC) Toronto Transit Commission (TTC) vehicles roam nearly 4,000 kilometres of safe, clean and convenient subway, bus, streetcar and light transit routes. One fare is usually all that's required on any one-way trip with no stopovers. Request transfers if you need to move between routes.

TTC services are available every day and some lines operate overnight (see Late Night Service page 28). On Sundays and holidays, a Family Pass ($7.00) gives you unlimited use of the entire system for up to two adults and four children. An unlimited Day Pass ($7.00) is available every day for individuals. Regular adult cash fare for all TTC services is $2.00. For detailed schedule and fare information, call 393-4636 (7–10, 7 days / wk) or visit www.city.toronto.on.ca.

The Regional Transit Ride Guide is a free publication provided through the TTC in Toronto. It is available from station fare collectors and the TTC Customer Centre at Davisville subway station. A larger version of the map is displayed in all subway and RT stations and City of Toronto transit shelters. In addition to TTC routes and fares, the Guide includes information for Brampton, Markham, Mississauga, Richmond Hill, and Vaughan. Government of Ontario (GO) Transit information is also included.

Subway and Light Rail Transit (LRT) Trains: On weekdays and Saturdays, trains run every few minutes from about 6 am until 1:30 am. On Sundays, they run from about 9 am to 1:30 am.

Buses and Streetcars: Most buses and streetcars start at about 5 am and run to about 1:30 am on weekdays, with reduced service on weekends and holidays. Buses and streetcars are equipped with route and destination information signs. Schedule information is posted at most major stops. Take care to look to your right when exiting onto the street.

Late Night Service: The Blue Night Network runs overnight on most major routes from about 1:30 am to 5 am every day. Transit stops are marked with a reflective blue band. Service is provided every 30 minutes or better.

GO TRANSIT Take the GO Train or GO Bus in and around Toronto. Trains run to various points around the city every day and evening. It's possible to stop here and there along the way. Try an economical day pass. For destination and schedule information use GO Transit's recorded information service 24 hours a day, or speak to a telephone information guide, on weekdays from 7 to 10 and weekends and statutory holidays from 9 to 7. Contact GO for information at (869-3200, Toronto local calling area, 1-888 GET ON GO 438-6646 long distance toll-free, TTY teletypewriters only at 1-800-387-3652) or www.gotransit.com. GO Transit's

Customer Service Centre (Union Station, 140 Bay St. weekdays 7 am–8 pm, weekends and holidays 10–6).

BUSES The Toronto Coach Terminal (610 Bay St.) has bus connections to many Canadian and American destinations.
Greyhound (367-8747). Buses across Canada and the territories from British Columbia to Quebec, but not east of Montreal. Also buses to USA destinations.
Trentway-Wagar (393-7911). Buses across Ontario with connections to Buffalo and Montreal.
Pacific Western Airport Shuttle (1-800-387-6787).
Ontario Northland (65 Front St. W., Union Station, 393-7911). Travel to Ontario's northern regions. Kiosk near main ticket window.

TRAINS Trains arrive and depart from Union Station at 65 Front W. for Canadian and international destinations.
VIA Rail (Union Station, 366- 8411 or toll free 1-888 VIA RAIL (842-7245), www.viarail.ca). VIA Rail offers discounts if you book five days in advance.
Amtrak (1-800-872-7245). Travel to, from and within the USA. Trains leave from Union Station.
Ontario Northland (Union Station. 304-0058 or 1-800-363-7512).Travel to Ontario's northern regions. Kiosk near main ticket window.

Arriving at Pearson Airport

Lester B. Pearson International Airport (905-676-3506), situated in the northwest corner of Toronto, is Canada's major gateway for domestic and international flights. Pearson's three terminal buildings are undergoing major renovations for future ease of accessibility. The airport is accessible by TTC, bus shuttles and major highways. Allow approximately 45 minutes to travel between the airport and downtown for a shuttle bus, or 1 hour by the TTC. The Traveller's Aid Society has a booth in each terminal which can provide useful information for visitors.

It is a good idea to arrive at least one hour before domestic flights and two hours before international flights.

Getting to Know Toronto: Its Natural and Social History

Tucked between the Oak Ridges Moraine and Lake Ontario, Toronto has a rich and fascinating natural history. It is a city shaped by its surroundings. From the early indigenous settlements to the multicultural diversity we live in today, Toronto has a rich and fascinating social and political history. It is the story of a people shaped by its ever-shifting context.

What follows is a broad brush stroke highlighting turning points in Toronto's natural and social history. There's so much more to read up on (see page 6) and so much to explore and understand once you get here. But for the time being …

The Land

For most of the last two million years glacial sheets dominated the northern hemisphere. Intermittent thaws stirred continents of ice to recede and revive. Pushing, pulling, and raking at the land, they consumed anything in their path. They swallowed mountains whole, the action of their bulk digesting them, grinding and crushing until nothing was left but thousands of years worth of boulders, gravel, clay, sand and silt. Over and over again, glaciers deposited sediment during retreat and engulfed it again on return, alternately concealing and unveiling new land masses and lake beds as though, dissatisfied with their creations, they needed to erase all evidence and start again.

Locally, glacial Lake Iroquois reached inland to the north along a line from about Finch in the east end, down to the current shoreline, along to Scarborough Bluffs and back up a winding course to follow Davenport Rd. before veering north and then south again on its way out of town to the west. When ice choking the St. Lawrence River relinquished its stranglehold, waters ebbed revealing the Lake Ontario of today.

The Wisconsin Ice Age was the last to cover Ontario, ending only ten thousand years ago. As two icy tongues of the Laurentide Ice Sheet withdrew, they filled a trench between them with gravel and sand, creating a ridge up to 300 metres high, from fifteen to twenty-five kilometres wide, running parallel to Lake Ontario's shoreline about

60 kilometres to the north. Named the Oak Ridges Moraine, it stretches from the Niagara Escarpment in the west to Rice Lake and the Trent River system in the east, ribbonning for nearly 200 kilometres of hilly kames and hummocky kettles with 34 watersheds running from it both north and south.

The Moraine is home to rare and endangered vegetation and wildlife. Over 130 bird species breed on the Moraine and another 60 pass through during migration. Its many varieties of plant life attest to the Moraine's fertility. Terrain features sandy plains, upland forests, kettle lakes, boggy wetlands, cedar swamps and ponds, extensive meadows, and even tall-grass prairie. This is a recreational wonderland for hikers, bikers, trekkers, skiers, birders, and explorers. Yet, hidden deep below ground is its most precious life source.

Moraines are composed of till, which is a mixture of clay, silt, sand, and stone. This till filters and controls the flow of water. The Oak Ridges Moraine is Southern Ontario's rain barrel and Toronto's largest ground water resource.

Unfortunately, inappropriate land-use on and below the surface of the Moraine is resulting in irreversible damage to the ecosystem of Southern Ontario. Garbage dumps, air pollution, deforestation, and rampant urban development all combine to interrupt natural cycles and rhythms. This resource is only renewable if left to its own devices. No one knows how much interference the system can tolerate before reaching a point of no return.

After years of encroachment, it is only now being recognized that the Oak Ridges Moraine needs protection. Still, there is no consensus on its future among the political, industrial, and other land use forces involved. But of one thing we can be sure, continuing misuse plays out like a game of Russian Roulette. Six Oak Ridges Moraine watersheds (those of the Highland, Etobicoke and Mimico Creeks, and the Humber, Don and Rouge Rivers) pass through or around Toronto and are fundamental to its environmental survival. Their ravines and those of their tributaries provide places of rare natural beauty and escape from the city. Highly sensitive, they harbour the vulnerable plant and animal life that depends on their waters and shelter. In many cases the watersheds have been suffering.

Unfettered urbanization has created environmental chaos. The natural balancing process in the watersheds cannot keep up with, and may never fully recover from, the onslaught of increasing demands to handle burdens. Urban surface water runoff, industrial waste, storm sewer overflow, ever-expanding road and other automobile infrastructure all exact a toll. And to the Moraine's additional detriment, we have interfered with its natural water courses.

The Don River, for example, originally meandered casually through its valley, and, to this day, you can still find evidence of the many little oxbow ponds it formed on its way. Two hundred years ago, it spilled into Lake Ontario through five separate mouths around small islands and deltas.

Eventually, in the name of progress and planning, it was channelled into a straight line. The creation of this line led directly to catastrophic annual flooding. Lesser waterways that we didn't like, we swept under an urban carpet. Garrison Creek (see page 54) and Taddle Creek (see page 79) were buried underground. Polluted and diverted, they eventually became channelled into our sewer system and covered over to prevent disease and to provide more land upon which to build. Renforth Creek in Coronation Park was dammed but you can still see its surface in the park reservoir. If the watershed lands don't survive, we lose more than beauty, we will lose a unique array of rich and varied plant and animal life.

Toronto is a meeting place for ecosystems. Here, Great Lake-St. Lawrence and Carolinian forest types meet. Vegetation includes trilliums (the Ontario provincial flower), trout lilies, sassafras, dogwood and wild hyacinth. Some plant life that exists side by side here, does so no where else in the world. Animal life thrives in the form of coyote, fox, and Blanding's Turtles, along with squirrels, chipmunks and racoons. Toronto is a major flyway and nesting area for many migrating birds, and year-round species like peregrine falcons and red-tail hawks are evident as well as pigeons, sparrows, and starlings.

Environmental sensitivity and stewardship is needed at every level, for every aspect of natural space in Toronto. Much is being done to protect the environment and reclaim what has been damaged or lost, but much more is needed. Many resource groups (see page 151) can assist you in learning about important environmental issues in Toronto, and give you opportunities to get involved.

The People

The story of Toronto as a city usually begins with the story of European settlement. However, Europeans were by no means the first human presence on and around these lands. Since the end of the last ice age almost 10,000 years ago, indigenous peoples have lived all along the Lake Ontario shore. The late 17th-century marked the arrival of the Huron, along with the Ahnishnabe and the Iroquois Confederacy, the last aboriginal groups to settle the land. These early inhabitants gave it the name Toronto ("meeting place" in the Huron language).

Here existed a defensible harbour, plenty of food, and abundant fresh water. The site made a natural base from which to access the network of essential trade routes formed by waterways and trails connecting Lake Ontario to the rest of North America. Upon arrival, the French used these same routes to expedite the flow of furs on the way to Europe. So ideal were the paths and trails that portions of Danforth (see page 100), Davenport Rd., Dundas St. W. (see page 67) and Kingston Rd. are built over their original course. Similarly, the old road along the Scarborough Bluffs (see page 120) and part of Gerrard St. E. follow routes at least 10,000 years old.

The French recognized the strategic military advantages here and the favourable position as a base camp for the fur trade. Keeping the name Toronto, they made maps of the area and built a fort at the mouth of the Humber River. The first European baby born here was to the wife of French settler Jean Baptiste Rousseaux (a plaque detailing the Rousseaux history can be found on South Kingsway, just north of The Queensway on the site of the original Fort York). When the British arrived, the family, baby in arms, was there to meet them.

In 1793, the British staked out an eight-street grid near today's St. Lawrence Market (see page 49), creating the nucleus around which Toronto would eventually form. They put their cultural stamp soundly upon Upper Canada by defeating the French in North America, and later fending off the Americans in the War of 1812. The grid was christened "Town of York" by the British but regained its original name of Toronto on its incorporation in 1839.

On its march into the twentieth century, Toronto became a bastion of the British way of life abroad.

Everything from historical buildings to street names affirms that Toronto was as Victorian as it could possibly be. In spite of a persistent independent streak, Toronto was colonial in every way. In 1837, the Upper Canada Rebellion forever changed Canada's relationship with England. However, the fight wasn't about escaping British ties, it was about self-determination within the embrace of the Empire. Even the British North America Act, which established the Dominion of Canada, was maintained in England and could only be changed by an act of British Parliament.

Upon entering the twentieth century, not even two world wars and a ruinous depression could check Toronto's explosive growth in population. Immigrants from all over the world made the city their home. A stronghold for those of British lineage in the mid-1900s, by 1970 they were in the minority. Canada's self-image as a fully independent nation was fully realized in 1982 when Britain relinquished its hold on our constitution making future changes the right of Canada's parliament.

Define Toronto today? It is a 24-hour-a-day city of hearty winters and long, hot summers that has something for everybody. It's a city that prizes cultural diversity and eschews the melting pot. It's a high energy city that has grown helter-skelter. Evolving first as a jumble of abutting, self-interested municipalities, later reinvented as a loose metropolitan grouping, and finally amalgamated as a "mega-city", Toronto continues to grow with spirit and intensity.

Responding to the dangers facing Toronto's environmental survival, action groups and concerned citizens have fomented social and political upheaval with revolutionary zeal. The reaction against the invasion of more expressways into downtown, the outrage against the deterioration of local ecosystems, and the fight to save the Oak Ridges Moraine (see page 31) and more recently the hot and heavy Adams Mine garbage debate, all demonstrate that people here are not afraid of a good social or political scuffle.

From this guide book, you'll see that Toronto has achieved quite a bit in the struggle to ensure a sustainable and unprejudiced social, economic, and environmental balance. Where more effort is needed, our Resource Groups section (see page 151) points the way to those poised for action. Welcome to our city, our town, our settlement by the lake.

Exploring the Other Side of Toronto

GETTING THE BIG PICTURE

Tours

Taking a tour is always a great way to orient yourself to the big picture. The good news is, you have quite a selection of green and "other" tours to choose from. We've listed some below:

Walking & Biking Tours / Organizations

Walking and biking — How much greener could you get? There are so many choices of walking and cycling tours in Toronto, it may be time to polish your walking shoes, oil your bike chain or rent a bike (see page 27).

Discovery Walks: The City of Toronto has created a wonderful series of self-guided walks, linking ravines, parks, gardens, beaches and neighbourhoods. Each walk is accessible by TTC and informative signs mark the route. Explore Toronto on foot and discover local area natural and social history, and during the warmer weather, see the many beautiful floral displays at feature park sites. Call 392-1111 for info and pamphlets or visit www.city.toronto.on.ca/parks. (Check out pages 54, 97, 118, 126, 131, 136, and 137 for more detailed descriptions).

A STROLL IN THE PARK (484-9255, www.interlog.com/~walktalk/). This nature lover's club organizes fun walks in Toronto's scenic parks all year.
A TASTE OF THE WORLD — NEIGHBOURHOOD BICYCLE TOURS & WALKS INC. (923-6813). Offers thematic walking and cycling tours that explore neighbourhoods, diverse cultures and ghostly haunts.
TORONTO BICYCLE NETWORK (766-1985, www.tbn.on.ca). Tours of Toronto and environs by bike.
HERITAGE TORONTO (392-6827 x 230, 233 or 256). Volunteer-led, free guided walking tours through many Toronto neighbourhoods from April to October.
MORE THAN JUST WALKING (701-1515, www.members.home.net/walking). Fitness walking club with a social aspect offering weekday power walks and weekend leisurely strolls.

NORTH TORONTO GREEN COMMUNITY (781-7663). Discover Toronto's natural history and take a Lost River tour.

RIVERDALE COMMUNITY BUSINESS CENTRE (462-0496). Historic walking tours of Riverdale.

ROM (ROYAL ONTARIO MUSEUM) WALKS (586-5513). Offers a variety of tours including heritage and other secrets of the city.

SCARBOROUGH CITY WALKERS (299-4575). Weekly walks in various parks in Scarborough.

TORONTO HEALTHY PARTNERSHIP (396-5656). Walking tour maps and guide information on walking tours in North York, Scarborough, East York and Etobicoke.

TORONTO FIELD NATURALISTS (593-2656). Offers tours of the Don River, High Park and the Rouge River.

WEST TORONTO JUNCTION HISTORICAL SOCIETY (763-3161, www.junctionhistory.on.ca). Heritage organization for the Junction neighbourhood hosts walking tours.

Other Tours

For other non-walking and non-biking tours see our Member Listings (page 155). Also check Tourism Toronto (page 18). Or check one of the many visitor information locations listed on page 18.

Attractions

Many attractions listed in the guide have their own tours or programs to offer. See the contact information under each listing.

Festivals and Events

Whatever the season, Toronto is hopping with festivals and events. We've listed some below, but make sure to check the weeklies for complete listings.

Toronto hosts many different film festivals including environmental, international, dance, gay and lesbian, fringe, children's and others. Check local papers like NOW and EYE or try Toronto.com. (See page 18.)

Year-Round

HARBOURFRONT CENTRE (235 Queens Quay W. at Lower Simcoe, 973-3000, www.harbourfront.on.ca).

Pick up a copy of their brochure at most visitor information centres and accommodations. Great multicultural and multi-ethnic festivals and events happen there frequently and many are free.

NATHAN PHILLIPS SQUARE at Toronto City Hall. (100 Queen W. at Bay, 392-0458, www.city.toronto.on.ca/special_events/nps.htm). In the centre of the city, the square is always bustling with people enjoying daily concerts, events, outdoor exhibitions, a farmers' market one afternoon a week in summer, children's events and skating in winter.

MEL LASTMAN SQUARE (5100 Yonge, north of Sheppard, 395-7350, www.city.toronto.on.ca/special_events/lastman_square htm). A dynamic city-run space surrounded by The Ford Centre for the Performing Arts, shops, and restaurants. The square hosts free events year round.

NOW and **EYE** magazines list events weekly. They're available free at bookstores, subway stations, restaurants and newspaper boxes on the street.

PEOPLE AND PLANET-FRIENDLY EVENTS & RESOURCES (www.planetfriendly.net). An email newsletter providing weekly info on green events and listings. Easy to subscribe and unsubscribe.

www.toronto.com and **www.torontofestivals.com** are good on-line sources of information.

Winter (November – February)

FIRST NIGHT (December 31), 973-3000 (from December 1st to 31st only), www.toronto.com. Alcohol-free, family-oriented New Year's Eve celebrations.

CHINESE NEW YEAR (between Jan 20 and Feb 12). This annual lunar festival is a huge community celebration.

WINTERFEST (February). Ice shows, performances, children's entertainers, free pancake breakfasts, giant midways, "make and take" crafts and much more.

CANADA BLOOMS (March), www.canadablooms.com. Canada's largest annual indoor flower and garden show.

Spring (March – May)

EARTH DAY EVENTS (April), www.earthday.ca. Check local listings for how to help save the planet

IMAGES FESTIVAL OF INDEPENDENT FILM AND VIDEO (April), 971-8405 www.interlog.com/~images/.

HOT DOCS (April/May), www.hotdocs.ca/. Canadian International Documentary Festival

FORSYTHIA FESTIVAL (May). This delightful springtime children's festival in Cabbagetown features a "kids and pets only" parade.

MILK INTERNATIONAL CHILDREN'S FESTIVAL (May), 973-3000. North America's largest festival of arts for young people.

FESTIVE EARTH SPRING FAIR (May), 469-2977. Celebrates and features environmental lifestyle events and an eco marketplace.

MAYWORKS FESTIVAL OF WORKING PEOPLE AND THE ARTS (May), 599-9096.

SLAW FESTIVAL (May), 921-3406. A "cabbagy" takeoff of the "Shaw Festival" (a nearby theatre institution) put on by the Cabbagetown Theatre Company, an amateur community theatre with professional polish.

CONTACT PHOTOGRAPHY FESTIVAL (May), 539-9595, www.contactphoto.com. A festival of exhibits, lectures, events, and open studios across the city throughout the month.

INSIDE OUT FESTIVAL (May), 925-9872 x 2229, www.insideout.on.ca. Toronto's Gay and Lesbian film and video festival.

BIKE WEEK (May), 392-7592, www.city.toronto.on.ca/cycling. Celebrates bicycle culture.

Summer (June –August)

RIDE FOR HEART (1st weekend in June), 486-RIDE (486-7433). About 4,000 cyclists ride up the temporarily car free Don Valley Parkway to raise money for heart and stroke research.

DESH PARDESH (June), http://home.ican.net/~desh/. A festival of South-East Asian culture.

GAY PRIDE PARADE (June), www.torontopride.com. More than 500 people volunteer their time to make Pride Day one of the city's and North America's largest street celebrations.

LESBIAN AND GAY PRIDE WEEK (June), www.torontopride.com. A celebration of lesbian, gay, bisexual, transsexual and transgendered culture.

SPLICE THIS! (June), www.interlog.com/%7Ecoldsore/. A super-8 film festival.

CANADA DAY (July 1). Anniversary of our nation's confederation. Events are held at various locations throughout Toronto. Check weeklies and www.toronto.com for up-to-date information.

SCREAM IN HIGH PARK (1st or 2nd Monday in July), www.scream.interlog.com. Featuring writers, performance artists, and the "carnival of the spoken word".
TORONTO OUTDOOR ART EXHIBITION (2nd week in July), 392-0458. A huge outdoor art exhibit at Nathan Phillips Square. Free.
THE FRINGE: TORONTO'S THEATRE FESTIVAL (July), 966-1062, www.fringetoronto.com. Annual summer theatre festival running for more than 12 years. Features hundreds of shows in various venues throughout the Annex. Check local listings for full details.
DREAM IN HIGH PARK (July/August), 367-8243 x 500. Pay what you can for this evening Shakespearean delight in High Park's outdoor theatre.
CARIBANA (late July/early August), www.toronto.com/caribana/. Caribbean music, dance, arts and crafts, fashion and food. Great parade held along the western lakeshore and other colourful events held on Olympic Island.
BEACHES JAZZ FESTIVAL (End of July or early August), 698-2152. Part of Queen St. E. is closed for outdoor and indoor jazz performances allowing for impromptu dancing in the streets.
SUMMERWORKS (August), www.summerworks.ca. A week-long theatre festival on the heals of the Fringe.
FRINGE FESTIVAL OF INDEPENDENT DANCE ARTISTS (Ffida) (August), 410-4291, www.ffida.org. Features local, national and international performers.
TASTE OF THE DANFORTH (August), 469-5634. Celebration of Greek culture and food over a three-day weekend. Attracts over 700,000 visitors.

Fall (September – October)

THE CABBAGETOWN FESTIVAL (September), 921-0857. One of Canada's oldest community festivals. The neighbourhood works together to make this colourful and exciting event a must for the whole family. Events include an arts and crafts show, a tour of elegant houses, a film and video festival.
AIDS WALK (September), 340-WALK (340-9255). Walkers raise money for AIDS research and organizations.
TORONTO INTERNATIONAL FILM FESTIVAL (mid-September), 967-7371. Now considered by the world press to be the most prominent film festival in the world. Over 900 screenings in 10 days.

WORD ON THE STREET (last Sunday of September), 504-7241. Part of Queen St. W. is closed to cars for this outdoor book and magazine festival celebrating the written word.
HARVEST FESTIVAL IN HIGH PARK (October), 392-6919. Traditional fall fair at **Colborne Lodge**.
CIBC RUN FOR THE CURE (October), https://www.cbcf.org/cibcrunforthecure/. Five kilometre run to raise funds for the Canadian Breast Cancer Foundation.
UNITED WAY CN Tower Stair Climb (3rd weekend in October), 761-STEP (761-7837), www.stairclimb.org. A fitness challenge to climb the 1,776 stairs in the world's highest free-standing structure organized to raise funds for the United Way.
PLANET IN FOCUS (October), www.planetinfocus.org. Canada's first international environmental film & video festival. Festival films highlight resourcefulness of concerned citizens and organizations in addressing social and environmental issues, and point towards creative solutions and hope for the future.
FALL SALMON RUN (2nd–3rd week of October). Coho Salmon swim upstream in the Rouge River.

Arts and Nightlife

Toronto has a hot theatre, dance, and music scene. Here are some sources to help you get the information you need to have a big Toronto night out.

Find Out More…

NOW MAGAZINE (See page 18.)
EYE (See page 18.)
TORONTO.COM (www. toronto.com, see page 19).
HARBOURFRONT CENTRE (973-3000, www.harbourfront.on.ca).
SLATE - ART MAGAZINE (www.slateartguide.com).
STRIDE ART AND GALLERY GUIDE (stride@sympatico.ca).
WHOLE NOTE (323-2232, www.thewholenote.com). Toronto music, classical & new music.
EXCLAIM! MAGAZINE (535-9735, www.exclaim.ca/). Free music reviews and listings in CD shops and bars.
TORONTO FESTIVAL ALLIANCE (111 Chesnut Cres., www.torontofestivals.com/nav.html).

FESTIVALS INFORMATION HOTLINE (968-FILM, 968-3456).
BALLET CREOLE (1443 Bathurst, 960-0350).

Information on Free Public Concerts

HARBOURFRONT CENTRE (www.harbourfront.on.ca). (See page 36.)
NATHAN PHILLIPS SQUARE and **MEL LASTMAN SQUARE** Event Hotline 395-7350 or 392-0458.

Ticket Sales and Concert Information:

You can get ticket information for a wide variety of theatre, dance, comedy and music events from the following sources:
T.O. TIX Toronto's half-price ticket outlet. (Toronto Eaton Centre — Mews level, Recorded message: 536-6468 x 40, www.culturenet.ca/tta). Half-price tickets only available by going there in person the day of the performance. Tickets for Sunday and Monday performances are sold on the preceding Saturday.
TICKETKING (872-3333, www.ticketking.com).
TICKETMASTER (870-8000, www.ticketmaster.ca).

Toronto has eight Festival Cinema locations showcasing mainstream and alternative films at discount rates. The bonus is that the cinemas are often in older art deco buildings. $7.50 for non-members, $4 for members. A bi-monthly Festival Guide is available at www.festivalcinemas.com or call 690-2000.

- **Fox Theatre, 2236 Queen St. E. at Beech Ave. 691-7330.**
- **Kingsway Theatre, 3030 Bloor St. W. at Royal York Rd. 690-2600.**
- **Music Hall, 147 Danforth Ave. at Broadview Ave. 778-8163.**
- **Paradise Cinema, 1006 Bloor St. W. at Westmoreland Ave. 690-2600.**
- **Revue Cinema, 400 Roncesvalles Ave. at Howard Park Ave. 690-2600.**
- **Royal Cinema, 606 College St. at Grace St. 516-4845.**

DOWNTOWN TORONTO

The Essence

The heart of this city is friendly. Still, it has a big city mentality. If you don't make the first move to make contact, everyone will pretty much respect your privacy and jostle around you as you try to keep track of directions. Remember, the lake is south and the CN Tower (see below) is near Union Station (see page 29), close to the lake.

We've organized the downtown information as if you arrived at Union Station. Yonge St. constitutes the dividing line between east and west. we start at the bottom with Front St. and explore first west, then east. We'll do the same with each major street northward to Bloor St. and then go back to the source with Toronto's waterfront and the two major river systems.

Where things don't fit neatly, we'll take some liberties so you don't miss anything.

The Roots — A Taste of History

In its earliest days, the city huddled around Front E. and Jarvis near the St. Lawrence Market, in an area now known as Old Town (see page 47). With the construction of Yonge, Toronto grew as merchants relocated to the new street to be close to traffic entering and leaving town. Expanding west, the city centred itself farther north on Yonge St. and the lakefront became largely industrial.

Front Street — Heading West

Heading west from Yonge, Front is home to some architectural giants. The old Post Office Building dominates the south west corner at Yonge Street. At one time all the mail heading into town was sorted there. On the north west corner is an old faux-baroque bank building that now houses the Hockey Hall of Fame.

The entire south side of Front. from Bay. to York. is graced by Union Station, one of the most beautiful buildings of its kind in Canada. This is the intersection of the subway line and all rail transportation in and out of Toronto — a hub of sustainable transportation! A tunnel at the west end of Union Station leads to the Skydome and to the CN Tower. This needle-like building was erected in 1976 and is still the tallest freestanding structure in the world.

©Rosemary G. Hasner, TRCA

Humber River Pedestrian Bridge

©Rosemary G. Hasner, TRCA

Young anglers at Colonel Samuel Smith Park

©Rosemary G. Hasner, TRCA

Canoeing challenge on the Humber River

Boy greets fish

Sylvan splendour in the Don Valley

City of Toronto Urban Development Services slide library

City of Trees

Vincenzo Pietropaolo

City of Toronto Archives Heritage History Exhibit, File 4315-009-006 1994, Item 3-7 (Photography: Peter MacCallum)

Prince Edward Viaduct

Toronto Field Naturalists

Don Valley Brickworks - north slope

Toronto Field Naturalists

Don Valley Brickworks - wetlands

“Tree City” emerges at Parc Downsview Park

Bruce Mau Design Inc.

City of Toronto Urban Development Services slide library

Don River

Vincenzo Pietropaolo

Perennial garden at Riverdale Farm

Fairmont Hotels & Resorts

Royal York Hotel — rooftop herb garden

Vincenzo Pietropaolo

Palm House at Allan Gardens

Edward Wickson

"Spadina Summer Under All Seasons" at Dupont Station

City of Toronto Culture Division

Lupin blooms at Spadina Historic House and Gardens

City of Toronto Culture Division

Spadina Historic House and Gardens

City of Toronto Urban Development Services slide library

High Park in winter

Vincenzo Pietropaolo

Spirit of Spadina

Vincenzo Pietropaolo

Chinese New Year celebration

Vincenzo Pietropaolo

Chinatown at night

Vincenzo Pietropaolo

Little Italy

Vincenzo Pietropaolo

St. Lawrence neighbourhood

Vincenzo Pietropaolo

Nightfall at Ossington and Bloor

Vincenzo Pietropaolo

BCE Place — Heritage Court Atrium

Vincenzo Pietropaolo

Union Station — grand foyer

City of Toronto

Allan Gardens Conservatory

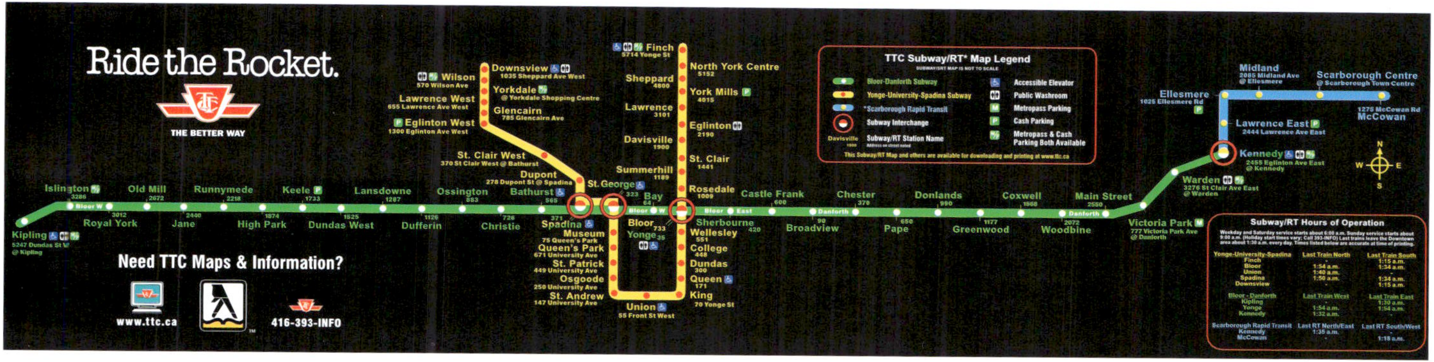
Ride the Rocket.
THE BETTER WAY
Need TTC Maps & Information?
www.ttc.ca
416-393-INFO
TTC Subway/RT* Map Legend
SUBWAY/SRT MAP IS NOT TO SCALE
Bloor-Danforth Subway
Yonge-University-Spadina Subway
*Scarborough Rapid Transit
Subway Interchange
Subway/RT Station Name
Accessible Elevator
Public Washroom
Metropass Parking
Cash Parking
Metropass & Cash Parking Both Available
This Subway/RT Map and others are available for downloading and printing at www.ttc.ca
Kipling
5247 Dundas St W
@ Kipling
Islington
Royal York
Old Mill
Jane
Runnymede
High Park
Keele
Dundas West
Lansdowne
Dufferin
Ossington
Christie
Bathurst
Spadina
St. George
Bay
Bloor
Yonge
Sherbourne
Castle Frank
Broadview
Chester
Pape
Donlands
Greenwood
Coxwell
Woodbine
Main Street
Victoria Park
777 Victoria Park Ave
@ Danforth
Warden
3276 St Clair Ave East
@ Warden
Kennedy
2455 Eglinton Ave East
@ Kennedy
Lawrence East
2444 Lawrence Ave East
Ellesmere
1025 Ellesmere Rd
Midland
2085 Midland Ave
@ Ellesmere
Scarborough Centre
@ Scarborough Town Centre
McCowan
1275 McCowan Rd
Finch
5714 Yonge St
North York Centre
Sheppard
York Mills
Lawrence
Eglinton
Davisville
St. Clair
Summerhill
Rosedale
Wellesley
College
Dundas
Queen
King
Union
55 Front St West
St. Andrew
147 University Ave
Osgoode
250 University Ave
St. Patrick
449 University Ave
Queen's Park
671 University Ave
Museum
75 Queen's Park
Dupont
278 Dupont St @ Spadina
St. Clair West
370 St Clair West @ Bathurst
Eglinton West
1300 Eglinton Ave West
Glencairn
785 Glencairn Ave
Lawrence West
655 Lawrence Ave West
Yorkdale
@ Yorkdale Shopping Centre
Wilson
570 Wilson Ave
Downsview
1035 Sheppard Ave West
N
S
E
W
Subway/RT Hours of Operation
Weekday and Saturday service starts about 6:00 a.m. Sunday service starts about 9:00 a.m. (Holiday start times vary. Call 393-INFO) Last trains leave the Downtown area about 1:30 a.m. every day. Times listed below are accurate at time of printing.
Yonge-University-Spadina | Last Train North | Last Train South
Finch | - | 1:15 a.m.
Bloor | 1:54 a.m. | 1:34 a.m.
Union | 1:40 a.m. | -
Spadina | 1:50 a.m. | 1:34 a.m.
Downsview | - | 1:15 a.m.
Bloor - Danforth | Last Train West | Last Train East
Kipling | - | 1:30 a.m.
Yonge | 1:54 a.m. | 1:54 a.m.
Kennedy | 1:32 a.m. | -
Scarborough Rapid Transit | Last RT North/East | Last RT South/West
Kennedy | 1:35 a.m. | -
McCowan | - | 1:18 a.m.

DOWNTOWN

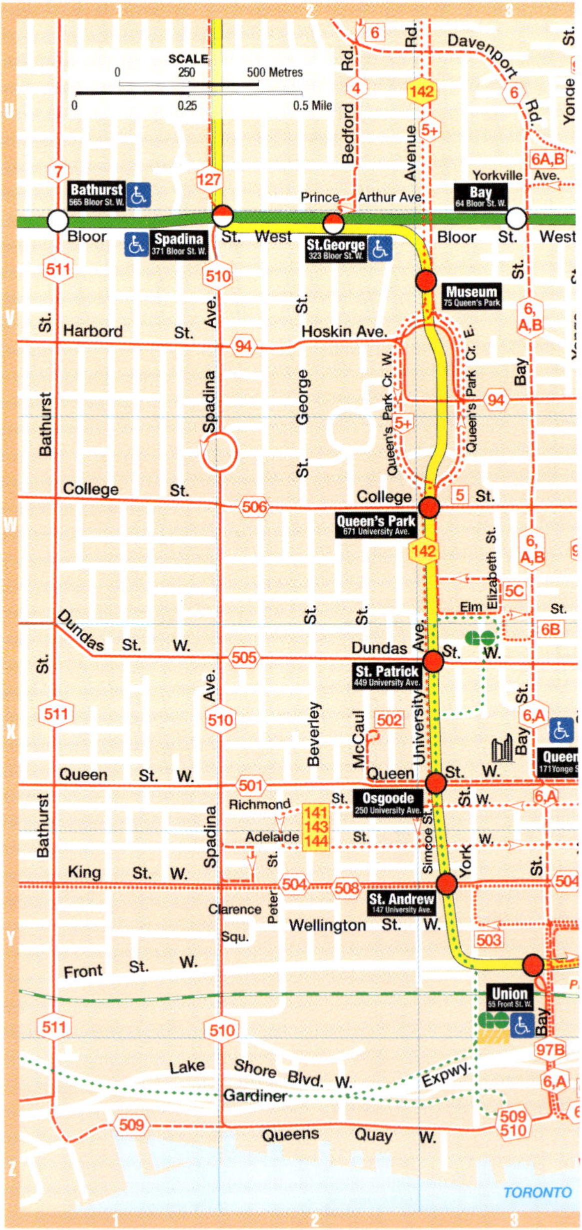

Yonge-University-Spadina Subway

Bloor-Danforth Subway

The Subway operates every few minutes from approx. 6:00am (9:00am Sundays) to 1:30am

75 **Regular Surface Routes**
(Bus, streetcar) Approx. 18-20 hours every day.

503 **Rush Hour Surface Routes**
Monday to Friday rush hours only from approx. 6:00-9:00am and 3:00-6:00pm

141

6

TORONTO

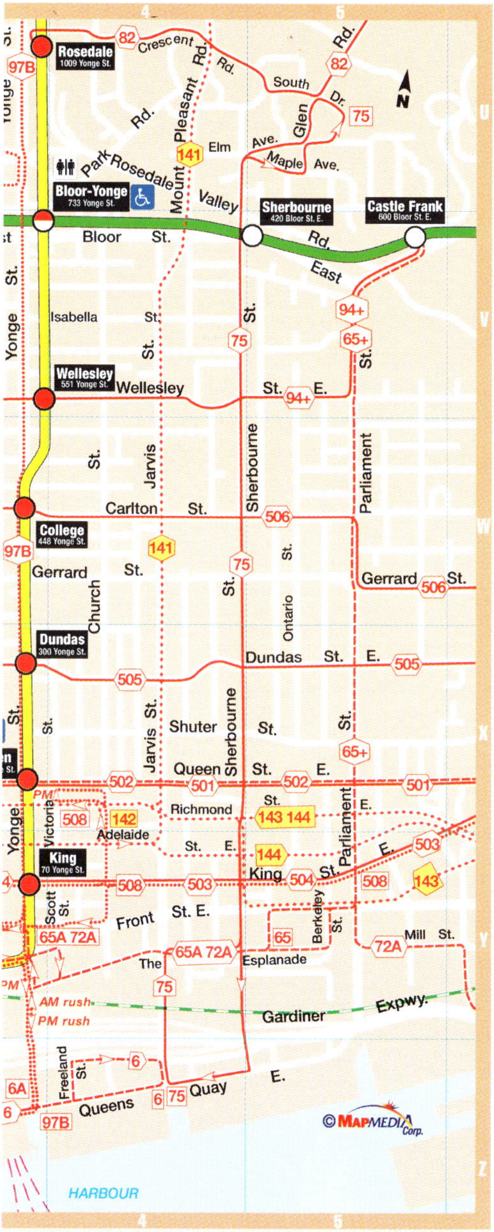

Premium Surface Routes — GO Rail Lines

Limited Service Surface Routes — Go Bus Express Lines

Service less than 18-20 hours every day, usually Monday to Friday from approx. 6:00am to 7:00pm with some evening and/or weekend service.

Accessible Elevator

A rectangular box indicates the end point of a line.

A pointed box is angled to indicate the direction of travel.

Arrows indicate the direction of travel around a loop.

A plus indicates that all route branches run along that portion of the route.

Cultural kaleidoscope — Harbourfront Centre

Cultural Festivals - Harbourfront Centre

Harbourfront map

Harbourfront Centre

Sunset on Lake Ontario

City of Toronto Urban Development Services slide library

Toronto Field Naturalists

Gibraltar Point Lighthouse on Centre Island

William Conway

Shoreline walkway - National Trade Centre, Exhibition Place

City of Toronto

Classic cruise on the Trillium paddleboat

City of Toronto Urban Development Services slide library

Sketcher's retreat on Algonquin Island

City of Toronto Urban Development Services slide library

Canada Geese foraging on Toronto Islands

Rosemary G. Hasner, TRCA

Cityscape from the Leslie Street Spit

Anne Tanner

Walking the labyrinth at Trinity Square Park

Vincenzo Pietropaolo

King's College Circle, University of Toronto

Vincenzo Pietropaolo

Painted Victorians in midtown Toronto

Andre Beneteau

Prospect Cemetery Mausoleum — stained glass

John Korec

Ukrainian Academy of Dance in Festival Parade

Eduard Sousa

Moss Park Community Garden before and after

Vincenzo Pietropaolo

Mount Pleasant Cemetery

Vincenzo Pietropaolo

R.C. Harris Filtration Plant

Gary Mulcahey

Corpus' Dusk Dances
Co-artistic directors Sylvie Bouchard & David Danzon

Vincenzo Pietropaolo

Bread baking in community oven in Dufferin Grove Park

Gibson House Museum

Culinary preparation at Gibson House

©Rosemary G. Hasner, TRCA

Timeless cycle at Black Creek Pioneer Village

Cliffhanger Productions – Stephanie Lake

The Fool's Whistle at the Guild Inn

©Rosemary G. Hasner, TRCA

Maple syrup time at the Kortright Centre

©Rosemary G. Hasner, TRCA

Walking through the wetlands at the Kortright Centre

Cedar Ridge Centre

Arcadian Landscape at Cedar Ridge Botanical Garden

Vincenzo Pietropaolo

High Park winterscape

City of Toronto

Bluffer's Park

The great green thing about the CN Tower is that from the top you can see why Toronto is called the City of Trees. Parks, ravines and the Toronto Islands dominate the panorama. It also makes an easy-to-see southern reference point. It houses the world's highest public observation tower at 447 m high off the ground.

The Skydome, home to the Toronto Blue Jays baseball team, is also used for a lot of really big-draw events. Similarly, the nearby Air Canada Centre shelters the Toronto Maple Leafs, one of the original six NHL Hockey Teams, and the Toronto Raptors NBA basketball team. Now you know where to go for big league sports.

If you decide to take in big league sports events, make sure you walk, bike or transit there and see if you can find a way to recycle your chilidog wrapper and juice can.

FRONT STREET WEST

Highlights

THE PATH Toronto's underground pedestrian tunnels form a network that connects much of the downtown through the lower levels of major buildings. For many years, a tunnel connected Union Station to the **Royal York Hotel**. When the Toronto Dominion Bank thrust its four inky towers skyward, it was decided to turn the below-ground level into networked corridors of shops and restaurants. Another corridor connected the complex to its neighbour on the south, the **Royal York Hotel**.

In a country blessed with snow, slush, and (in bygone days) mud, this convenience allows pedestrian-only access to the downtown and encourages walking. Now it is possible to come into town by train, stay at a luxury hotel and attend a meeting with your banker, all with easy walking access and away from car traffic.

The linked system of underground malls runs from Front St. to just north of Dundas Street. For guided tours of the PATH call Silk Path Tours at 410-1656 or find them on the web at www.toronto.com/silkpathtours.

While looking down on Toronto from the CN Tower's observation deck, you can count the growing number of green roofs. Each contributes to insulating and cooling the buildings, absorbing storm water and improving your view!

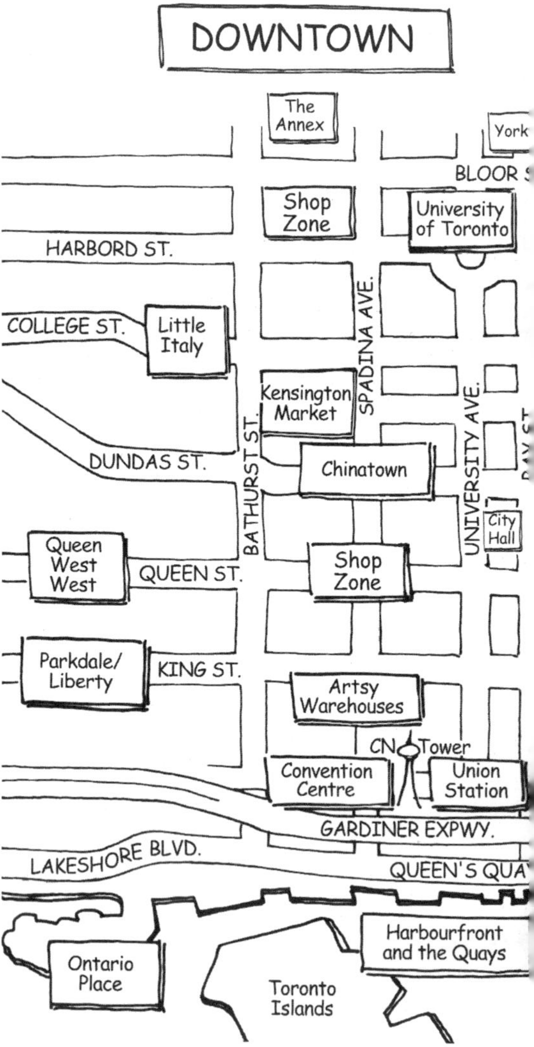

DOWNTOWN
The Annex
York
BLOOR
Shop Zone
University of Toronto
HARBORD ST.
SPADINA AVE.
COLLEGE ST.
Little Italy
Kensington Market
UNIVERSITY AVE.
BATHURST ST.
DUNDAS ST.
Chinatown
City Hall
Queen West West
QUEEN ST.
Shop Zone
Parkdale/ Liberty
KING ST.
Artsy Warehouses
CN Tower
Convention Centre
Union Station
GARDINER EXPWY.
LAKESHORE BLVD.
QUEEN'S QUA
Harbourfront and the Quays
Ontario Place
Toronto Islands

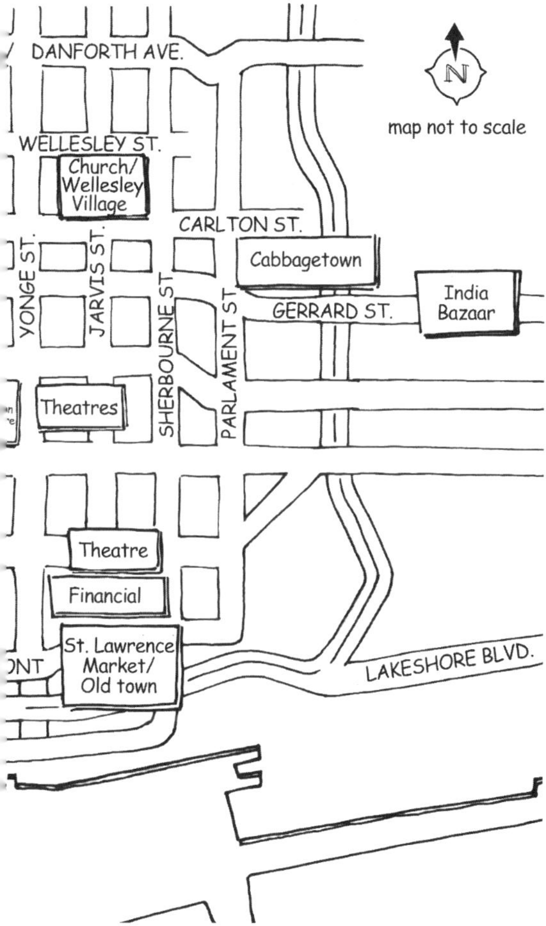
DANFORTH AVE.
map not to scale
N
WELLESLEY ST.
Church/ Wellesley Village
CARLTON ST.
YONGE ST.
JARVIS ST.
SHERBOURNE ST
PARLAMENT ST
Cabbagetown
GERRARD ST.
India Bazaar
Theatres
Theatre
Financial
St. Lawrence Market/ Old town
LAKESHORE BLVD.

ROYAL YORK HOTEL (100 Front W., 368-2511). When the hotel opened in 1929, it was the tallest building in the British Empire. For decades it was a distinctive feature of the Toronto skyline. In recent years it has taken upon itself the challenge to be an environmentally aware and active friend to the downtown.

A rooftop garden grows most of the herbs used in the hotel kitchen (see Photo section); hygiene and waste management procedures are environmentally sound; and guestroom products are environmentally safe. Although not the only downtown tourism business to take an environmentally friendly approach, this hotel was one of the first, and managed to set an outstanding example.

The Royal York's green program has reduced the hotel's landfill waste by 72% and water consumption by 181,600 litres. In 1998 the hotel donated $137,000 worth of food to the Second Harvest Program (408-2594), a not-for-profit food recovery program that distributes surplus perishable and prepared food. Over 990 kilograms (2,200 pounds) of organic waste per day, or 324 tonnes (360 tons) per year is pulped and fed to some 600 pigs rather than going into the garbage. Installation of newspaper disposal containers saved $18,700 and 144,045 kilograms (320,100 pounds) of paper. You can even take a tour of its recycling facilities.

The *Deep Lake Water Cooling (DLWC)* project is an innovative plan by the city of Toronto to draw the naturally cold lake water found deep in Lake Ontario through pipes to several downtown buildings for efficient air-conditioning and energy use reductions.[6]

ROUNDHOUSE PARK (At the foot of the CN Tower. Tour info: 868-6937). Have a walk and enjoy a beer — the Roundhouse is the place to do both. It is an extravaganza of green tourism from green space to energy conservation to sustainable transportation. This 6 hectare (15 acre) area features the Canadian Pacific John St. Roundhouse, a 1929 National Heritage Site. It is surrounded by an urban forest, beautiful in all seasons of the year. An aspen thicket and birch mound together with 400 trees including oak, red maple and eastern larch. This complements a prairie garden complete with flowers that require no watering, fertilizer or pesticides. A meadow features a mix of native grasses, wildflowers, and wildlife. It makes a lovely place to stroll or to play.

The John St. Roundhouse was the first to use a unique clean air and energy conservation system called the direct steam process — an environmental method that heats the 71-year-old building today. This is also where you will find the **Steam Whistle Brewery** (362-2337). Once all museum plans are approved, Steam Whistle will help raise funds to create a long-awaited Railway Museum to display the vintage steam locomotives currently housed in an adjacent part of the building.

Things to Do, See, Buy & Eat

HOCKEY HALL OF FAME (30 Yonge, BCE Place, 360-7765). If you like hockey, you'll love the paraphernalia in this beautifully restored Bank of Montreal building. This is a true Canadian tradition. Sports fans flock to the Hall over and over again.

BCE PLACE (Heritage Square Atrium, 161-181 Bay, 777-6480). This is an amazing mix of indoor and outdoor, heritage and new. Note the beautiful glass-ceilinged Galleria designed by Santiago Caltrava (25.5 meters / 85 feet high, 13.5 meters / 45 feet wide and 114 meters / 380 feet long). (See Photo section.)

CBC MUSEUM AND GLENN GOULD STUDIO (250 Front W., 205-3310). Some shows broadcast live from the impressive public lobby and recording hall. Toronto's own Bicycle Choir performed there once on bikes!

METRO TORONTO CONVENTION CENTRE (255 Front W., 585-8000). A hub of major conference and tradeshow activity. Be sure to ask about their recycling and food waste diversion programs.

Front Street — Heading East

Here is the birthplace of today's Toronto. Unfortunately, most of the historical buildings of Front E. are either gone or converted to commercial use and inaccessible to the public. Front E. is linked closely to King E. in respect to early Toronto history and landmarks. Look at both sections to develop an itinerary for the Old Town. It is a day-tripper's delight, defined by history, dining and shopping, all within a few compact blocks.

St. Lawrence Market and Old Town of York

The Essence

A vast, clamorous 19th-century market hall or intimate

bistro nightlife, which will it be today? Both, of course, with a liberal smattering of history. In fact, it's impossible to get through this neighbourhood without running up against a heritage building, or passing by a historical point of interest.

At Yonge and Front (west side stomping grounds to early settlers) stands the cavernous, 3,200-seat Hummingbird Centre, home of the National Ballet of Canada and the Canadian Opera Company. To the immediate east is the St. Lawrence Centre for the Arts, Hummingbird's diminutive neighbour, and home to the Canadian Stage Company. Canadian works predominate in its two theatres.

Like an ocean liner steaming east down Front, the 1891 Gooderham Building (also known as the Flatiron Building) is a custom fit to the triangle of land it occupies at the corner of Wellington and Church Streets. The building's west end holds a stunning trompe l'oeil suggesting that the building's entire back wall is being lifted away by the wind.

Daytime crowds are drawn to the St. Lawrence Market for fresh produce, fish, meat and for the European-style market ambience. Evenings are for theatre outings. More recently, people have flocked to the high-rise condominiums that fill just about every available space. With locals demanding more to do nearer to home, eateries, shops, and clubs are opening all the time alongside the neighbourhood's many antique markets.

The Roots — A Taste of History

At the end of the 18th century, the shoreline of Lake Ontario came right up to the halfway mark of today's St. Lawrence Market. Front fronted the water's edge. The Toronto of 1793 has now all but vanished, leaving just enough physical evidence to provide a basis from which to appreciate its life and times.

Imagine the rutted paths staked out as George, Berkeley, Adelaide and Front Sts., boundaries to the Town of York, capital of Upper Canada. Icy and treacherous by winter, they were sucking quagmires each spring, slowly hardened as they lay by each summer's sun. A trip out of doors was always an uncertain adventure.

Construction was slow to start, since most of the first arrivals were soldiers with few craftsmen among them. Next on the scene were bureaucrats; no craftsmen there. By 1810 brick structures included one house and one legislature building. One hundred wooden houses accommodated about 600 people.

The War of 1812 marked a boom period for York. Fortunes were made by merchants who saw military provisioning as an incentive to set up shop. War shortages created a seller's market. Entrepreneurs soon outnumbered bureaucrats and their aggressive spirit changed the fledgling community from a sedentary, civil-service backwater to a town of opportunity where limits for success were set largely by ambition to succeed.

In 1834 York was incorporated and chose as its new name, Toronto (as it had been known to past generations of native peoples). A court house, a jail, market buildings and churches sprang up. A fire hall and a school soon followed. But wooden buildings were the norm, and in 1849 a fire devastated the entire community. Stone and brick buildings that survived were restored and some are today's community highlights.

Perhaps it was a response to overcrowding, and marshy conditions, or maybe it was the fear of another inferno, but, as is still often the case, people of sufficient means began to build on the outskirts of town. Toronto flowed amoebae-like to the west and to the north, always ingesting more land.

When Governor General Simcoe built Yonge. as Toronto's access route to the north, merchants gravitated there and as everyone else followed, Toronto stood up, shuffled a few blocks west, sat down, and grew. To really get a feel for the heritage of the area take a walk around the historic St. Lawrence market starting at Union Station. Contact the city's heritage division for more information (392-6827 x 230).

Highlights

ST. LAWRENCE MARKET (91 Front E. at Jarvis, 392-7219). Open every day except Sunday and Monday, the Market is a smorgasbord of tastes, sights and sounds. Featuring fabulous foods from around the world (including organic produce), it is a hub of activity to delight the senses.

Since 1803, a thriving market has occupied these grounds. Captured in the façade of the current building is the unmistakable outline of a smaller building. This was our first City Hall. The market occupied the first floor with shops and offices in the wings. The second floor was the Council Chamber, and the police station was in the basement. When the politicians moved to a new City Hall some 40 years later, the market completely took over this site. It was at this time (1845) that the enclosing structure was added. In 1970, the second floor Council Chambers were renovated to create the **Market Gallery**.

MARKET GALLERY (95 Front E., 392-7604). This is the City of Toronto's official exhibition space. Displays here document the city's development through maps, photographs, documents, art and artifacts from the city's extensive archive collection. Special shows focus on aspects of the city's growth. Educational programs are available for groups, including presentations for English as a Second Language students.

The *St. Lawrence Centre Forum* is a free series of evening forums through the fall and winter that features discussion and debate on the life of the city. Guest speakers include national and local leaders in social, political and economic thought. Find them on the web at www.stlc.com\forums.htm, pick up a flyer at 27 Front St. E. or call 366-1656.

Things to Do, See, Buy & Eat

HUMMINGBIRD CENTRE FOR THE PERFORMING ARTS (1 Front E., 393-7469). Originally known as the O'Keefe Centre, this centre has seen much of Toronto's visiting arts and dance for the past 3 decades. Check out the mural.

EUROPE BOUND (49 Front E., 601-0854). Outdoor gear, bike rentals travel books, magazines and more.

TRAILHEAD (61 Front E., 862-0881). Outdoor gear (including summer rental of camping equipment, canoes & kayaks and cross-country skis in the winter).

C'EST WHAT? (67 Front E., 867-9499). This bar/restaurant promotes micro-brews and Ontario wine. It's bicycle-friendly and showcases local music.

VITAL PLANET HEALTH SHOP (92 Front E., 366-4353). Bulk & frozen organic food and dairy products and supplements.

ST. LAWRENCE MARKET COMPLEX AND FARMERS MARKET (92 Front E., North Market, 392-7120). Saturdays 5-5. Antiques and collectables market Sundays dawn to 5.

THE ESPLANADE AND FOOD MARKET One whole block of Front Street provides an abundance of outdoor eating.

Visitor Information

TRAVELLERS AID SOCIETY OF TORONTO
Union Station (See page 18.)

INFO TORONTO, METRO CONVENTION CENTRE
Front St. (See page 18.)

King Street — Heading West

King West is a chameleon. Where it intersects Bay it is the stodgy heart of the financial district. Then as it crosses University it dons the tie and tails of an entertainment maven. Before merging into the western tangle that becomes the Queensway, it plunges without pretension into the Parkdale/Liberty neighbourhood, one of Toronto's most inspiring arts communities.

Toronto celebrates over 180 performing arts companies and is the third largest host of English theatre in the world (after London and New York). In 1962, Toronto had only two professional live theatres! [7]

Highlights

DESIGN EXCHANGE (234 Bay, 216-2160). Housed in the historic former Toronto Stock Exchange (TSE) building, this unique centre promotes design as an important contribution to Canadian innovation. bringing together specialized skills and innovative approaches that support commercial, technical and scientific progress without sacrificing the economic, social or environmental health of our cities. It was officially opened in September 1994, by Canadian Prime Minister Jean Chrétien.

The moment you step inside, a marble grand-staircase draws you to the second floor. Here, amid art deco splendour, you are rewarded with eight breath-taking murals by renowned Canadian artist Charles Comfort depicting Canadian Industry in the 1930s.

Exhibition space for both large and small installations, competitions and special displays of innovative work emphasize the Design Exchange philosophy. A resource centre provides space for businesses, students and designers to do research.

Stop by the café for a coffee, or explore "Swipe", the Design Exchange store featuring a wide range of design books, innovative products, and one-of-a kind gifts.

THE ROYAL ALEXANDRA THEATRE (260 King W., 872-1212). Designed by John M. Lyle and completed in 1907, the theatre was named for King Edward VII's wife. Since then, it has seen everything from classical repertory to smash hit musicals. The dowager of Toronto theatres, it tucks under its belt over 3,000 productions, including performances by international stars like the Barrymores, Helen Hayes, Sir John Gielgud, Ralph Richardson, Allan Lunt, Margot Fontaine and Paul Robeson.

The Royal Alex was advertised as the continent's first fireproof and air-conditioned theatre. In 1963, when attendance hit a low ebb and the building was threatened with demolition, entrepreneur Ed Mirvish bought and restored the building to its full Edwardian splendour. Average ticket prices range from $25 to $75.

FINANCIAL DISTRICT
At King and Bay.

Peregrine falcons nest here. Perhaps they feel at home among the cliffs of commerce. 8

Things to Do, See, Buy & Eat

ST. ANDREW'S PRESBYTERIAN CHURCH (73 Simcoe, 593-5600). Built in 1874, it features quite a visually-remarkable interior.

ROY THOMSON HALL (60 Simcoe, 872-4255). Home to the Toronto Symphony Orchestra.

METRO HALL (55 John). This building houses various municipal offices. It won the 1995 Toronto Building of the Year (TOBY) award for its energy efficiency and accessibility by public transport. It also has a full recycling program, bicycle parking and free conference rooms for public consultation.

PRINCESS OF WALES THEATRE (300 King W., 872-1212). In this 2,000-seat house, celebration of current theatre technology, art work, murals and woodwork relief are special attractions.

KING BETWEEN JOHN & PETER Great restaurants with live jazz, music and patios in the summer. The variety of food here spans about four continents.

ART METROPOLE (788 King W., 2nd Fl., 703-4400). Contemporary art and artists' work displayed.

EUROPE BOUND (383 King W., 205-9992). Outdoor gear and equipment rentals and sales.

MOUNTAIN EQUIPMENT CO-OP (400 King W., 340-2667). Outdoor gear and equipment sales and rentals. This co-operative store helps save the earth through its environmental fund and has donated more than $150,000 to environmental projects and organizations.

PARI NADIMI GALLERY (80 Spadina, 4th Fl., 591-6464). Contemporary art exhibits.
IMAGINE (96 Spadina, 504-2379). Veggie food cafeteria style.
VEGETABLE KINGDOM ORGANICS & DELI (443 Adelaide W., 703-6447). Organic groceteria, mostly preservative-free goods.
ARTWORD THEATRE AND GALLERY (75 Portland, 408-2783). Performance art, readings, dance theatre and gallery.
AMSTERDAM BREWING COMPANY (600 King W., 504-1040). In the summer, enjoy a micro-brew on the patio oasis.

The Better Buildings Partnership (BBP) program, run by the City of Toronto, with support from Toronto Atmospheric Fund and energy companies, encourages local owners to improve the efficiency of their buildings to reduce energy and water use. For more info, visit www.city.toronto.on.ca/energy/building.

Parkdale / Liberty

The Essence

Away from the downtown core, along King W., you can sense the overpowering pull of a community making the old new again and turning adversity into opportunity. Parkdale is getting its second wind after years of fatigue and neglect. Adventurous entrepreneurs seize opportunities to animate the neighbourhood.

Overnight, vacant spots become thriving restaurants, clubs, studios, and galleries, embracing social, cultural, and economic diversity. Festivals and events affirm artistry, community, and heritage. Whether you're long on the scene, just visiting from nearby, or brand new to Canada, Parkdale makes room for you.

The neighbouring Liberty area, home to early industrial Toronto, is also coming to life after years of struggle and surrender. Commercial revitalization has been marked by the arrival of high-tech, multi-media and film companies.

Combined with the reincarnation of abandoned factories and office buildings as loft apartments and condos, this area is emerging as an attractive, busy, lively, and safe place to live, work, and play. More parks, better leisure options, and a broader range of recreational choices make this area home to many, and playground to many more.

The Roots — A Taste of History

In the late 1800s, Parkdale was a lakeside suburb for people escaping industrialized Toronto. Spacious homes on large tracts of property were the norm. The Liberty area, with handy rail and port access, evolved as a centre for light to medium sized manufacturing. Today, explorers can see the remnants of that era in the architectural grandeur of many of the old factory buildings now converted to residential and commercial use.

By the end of the 1950s, disruption and instability began to take its toll. Construction of the Gardiner Expressway cut off the neighbourhood from Lake Ontario, leaving it with inadequate parkland. Conversions of homes into flats, bachelor units and rooming houses attracted transient rather than permanent residents. Manufacturing moved to the suburbs, leaving many unemployed.

For many years, the neighbourhood languished while the rest of the city turned its back. It will take more time but, entering the twenty-first century, this community is slowly and deliberately picking up the social, economic and environmental pieces.

Highlights

GARRISON CREEK AND GARRISON COMMON. Up until 150 years ago, a sparkling creek gathered tributaries as it made its way from north of St. Clair Ave., down across old Davenport. through a deep-sided ravine, and into Lake Ontario. Along the creek at Garrison Common, **Fort York** (see page 112) was built in early 1793, signalling the beginning of the British presence that led to the establishment of Toronto. Near the south east corner of what is now Trinity-Bellwoods Park, an inlaid sidewalk map surrounded by the word "water" in 24 languages depicts the original course of Garrison Creek.

The Creek didn't fare as well as it should have. Once an excellent source of transportation and drinking water, it became a repository for industrial waste and garbage. Too polluted to be left open, it was buried in 1884 as part of a sewer system, and today flows underground. Subsequent landfill and paving leave only a suggestion of Garrison Creek's existence.

GARRISON CREEK DISCOVERY WALK (392-1111). The Garrison Creek Discovery Walk is about four kilometres long and takes you from Christie Pits on Bloor W. south to the Martin Goodman Trail (see page 105) by the lake. You can take side trips at any point en route and enjoy the hospitality of the many neighbourhoods edging the trail. The trail itself takes you on through Bickford, Harbord, and Fred Hamilton Parks to Roxton Rd. Parkette. Moving on south through Trinity-Bellwoods Park and Stanley Park brings you to **Fort York** and Garrison Common.

Things to Do, See, Buy & Eat

FACTORY THEATRE (125 Bathurst north of King at Adelaide, 504-9971). A café and theatre are housed in this beautiful Victorian Mansion.

ACADEMY OF SPHERICAL ARTS AND LA BELLE EPOQUE (38 Hanna, 532-2782). Lunch, dinner, and pool games. This circa 1890 building was once the home of the Brunswick Balke Collender Company and manufactured billiard equipment and accessories. It still has some ornate antique pool tables to play on.

MILDRED PIERCE RESTAURANT (99 Sudbury, 588-5695). Great décor, and a special treat, the menu changes according to season.

King Street — Heading East

To the east, King marks the northern boundary of the Town of York (to capture absolutely everything, we include Adelaide one block north). A full day's itinerary can easily be developed by combining elements here with other elements of Front Street East.

Highlights

TORONTO SCULPTURE GARDEN (115 King E). Ready for outdoor sculptural drama and dynamism against a botanical backdrop? We thought so. This small park is devoted to changing displays of thought provoking outdoor sculpture. Positioned as it is, a narrow sliver of open space in a densely built up street, don't blink or you'll miss it.

TORONTO'S FIRST POST OFFICE (260 Adelaide E., 865-1833). Opened in 1833 as the fourth post office in York, it became Toronto's first, after the city's incorporation. Serving a population of about 9,000, it was an important communications centre for the provincial capital.

In the years following its use as a post office, the

building variously served as housing, a boy's school, a biscuit factory, and a records centre. At one point, a farmer's co-operative organization operated it as a butter factory and egg storage facility. Joining the ranks of the neglected, the building deteriorated until 1978, when it was gutted by fire and faced demolition.

Along with neighbouring buildings it was saved by private investment. Now administered by the Town of York Historical Society, it operates as a sanctioned postal franchise and has its own distinctive historical cancellation stamp (so be sure to mail a postcard from here).

There is also an artist-in-residence program for the production of handmade paper, and workshops in papermaking are on offer from time to time. By appointment, costumed volunteers lead group tours and answer questions.

ENOCH TURNER SCHOOL HOUSE (106 Trinity, 863-0010). This perfectly intact building is maintained in the character of its day. Today, the Schoolhouse offers a chance to see how Canadian children were taught over a century ago.

For the first half of the 19th century, the working-class Protestant Irish of Toronto could not afford to send their children to school. The city fathers, although well aware of this crisis, balked at the prospect of public education. A local brewer, Enoch Turner, for whom many of the affected people worked, took action. He built a school. On land adjacent to Little Trinity Church, an audacious little building sprang up that combined the efforts of three architects.

In 1848, it welcomed children from some of the very poorest Toronto families and offered them a church-guided, co-educational, elementary level education for free. Free education was unheard of in the province at the time.

When the local school board took over in 1851, they were ill at ease with the idea of co-education, and uncomfortable with what they considered the undue influence of the church. By 1860, they had opened another school nearby that was appropriately segregated and public, as opposed to religious in nature. Entry is but visits are by appointment only.

Things to Do, See, Buy & Eat

COURT HOUSE GARDEN (Court west of Church near St. James Park). A reclaimed parking lot including sculpture and a rose and herb garden.

CATHEDRAL OF ST. JAMES & GARDENS (65 Church, east of the cathedral, 364-7865). Nestled beside the Cathedral is an exquisite formal floral sanctuary. Open dusk to dawn.

LITTLE TRINITY CHURCH (425 King E). Built in 1845 as an affordable church in times of expensive pew rentals. Loved by flower children of the 60s as the church of "the little guy".

Queen Street — Heading West

Queen Street at Yonge

Highlights

TRINITY SQUARE — EATON CENTRE. If you need an escape, don't overlook Trinity Square just off the Eaton Centre. Buy a great lunch at the Trinity Square Café (598-2010) which operates as a training program for people recovering from mental health problems. Munch while you contemplate the Labyrinth and enjoy the lovely water feature running from the south side of Trinity Square to Bay obliterates the sound of traffic. Queen at Yonge has always been considered the centre of town. As you move west to Bay and you meet the northern tip of the financial district and City Hall, the seat of Toronto government. Another couple of blocks and you exchange formal for funky. From University to Spadina, Queen is a great way to experience the best of urban organic chaos.

THE LABYRINTH — TRINITY SQUARE. A labyrinth is an ancient spiritual pattern for meditative walking. This one, a 23-metre (77-foot) diameter circular winding path, has been cut into the grass in the Trinity Square Courtyard. It is based on the pattern at Chartres Cathedral in France (see Photo section). Labyrinths are often built close to water, so it is auspicious that this one is built over the former course of Taddle Creek (see page 79). The Labyrinth provides a break from the hustle and bustle of the Bay and Queen surroundings.

CITY HALL(S) & NATHAN PHILLIPS SQUARE (100 Queen W., 392-9111). The half circle of two arched towers poised over a saucer-like central Council Chamber is Toronto's striking City Hall. It was designed by Viljo Revell and built in the early 1960s. Here, decisions on environmental, economic and social policy for Toronto are made.

Nathan Phillips Square hosts events and houses demonstrations year round. There is a bustle of activity every day at lunch and a cornucopia awaits all at the farmer's market held every Wednesday 10–2 from the early summer through the fall.

Inside City Hall you can get all kinds of information about what's happening in the city, or take in one of the ever-changing displays in the main rotunda.

Nathan Phillips Square is framed by an elevated walkway and surrounds a reflecting pool. The pool becomes a skating rink in winter complete with a skate rental shop on the premises. In the west corner of the Square a huge, challenging bronze sculpture fronts the City Hall building. Titled *The Archer*, it is the work of celebrated British sculptor Henry Moore. Much more of his work is on display at the Art Gallery of Ontario (see page 68).

Across Bay St, Old City Hall's imposing brickwork frontage bears down on the financial district as though keeping an eye on all those bankers. It survives today as a provincial courthouse. The George A. Reid murals just inside the doors commemorate Canadian pioneer life. Check out the exhibit cabinets on the main floor. They chronicle the movement to save the building from demolition when the Eaton Centre was being planned. Old City Hall is now protected as a National Historical Site.

Have you seen Toronto's sculpted wildlife? Look for the Metro Hall dogs, the Eaton Centre geese, and the TD Centre cows. In 2000, hundreds of life-sized fibreglass moose stood anchored throughout Toronto. Decorated by local artists, the herd was let loose on Toronto to provide a light-hearted glimpse of Toronto pride and community spirit.

CLOUD GARDENS (THE BAY ADELAIDE CONSERVATORY) (Northwest corner of Richmond W. at Yonge, 392-1111). Enter a tropical cloud forest in the heart of the financial district. These cloud forests are only naturally found in South America and parts of Southern Asia. The plant life here thrives in a controlled environment of moderate temperatures, high humidity, and abundant rainfall. Take a walk and experience a tropical climate in the city.

Things to Do, See, Buy & Eat

THE BAY (Yonge at Queen). The Hudson's Bay Company department store is a great Canadian legacy. With over

300 years of history it's Canadian through and through. For more info on the company's history and influence on Canada's evolution, visit www.hbc.com/hbchistory/.

OSGOODE HALL AND GARDENS (130 Queen W., 947-3300). You'll find beautiful gardens, a wrought iron cow gate and perfectly manicured grounds with benches for repose in front of this grand building, home to the highest court in the province.

The *Hilton Toronto Glass Elevator* is not as high as the CN Tower, but it's a free ride and you can get a good overview of west end downtown — if only a brief stay at the top.

Visitor Information

ACCESS TORONTO INFORMATION DESK. Visitor info available at City Hall. (See page 18.)

ONTARIO TRAVEL INFORMATION CENTRE. Toronto Eaton Centre. (See page 18.)

Want to know the weather? Look up at the Canada Life Building weather beacon — if the lights are going down the temperature is falling. If the lights are going up, the temperature is rising. If the box at the top is flashing red, it is going to rain. If it's green, it will be sunny. A flashing white box means snow. For more details, pick up an info card at 330 University (main lobby desk).

Queen Street West

From University to Spadina.

Whether you're looking for the components to make a particle accelerator, or just trying to find that elusive ingredient to turn hair a nice neon chartreuse, you'll find it here if you find it anywhere: an electronics shop next to a sushi bar, beside a natural soap store, across from a jazz emporium that has seen better days but never better music . . . as a neighbourhood, it's nothing if not eclectic. And then, of course, there's that television station, CITY TV, that likes nothing better than to drag celebrities out to the street for live interviews in front of mildly foaming-at-the-mouth crowds.

For the architecturally inclined, this street is, like Parkdale a little farther west, a two-faced street. Look at the high-tech storefronts with all the glitter and glitz, then, gaze up toward the roof lines and you're back in the early 1900s. But for the most part, it's all about those ground-level storefronts. Don't forget to sample one of the many funky cafés and restaurants. This is a place where daytime shoppers, browsers and noshers give way to after-dark ravers, punks, and club kids. Since the 1970s, the music scene has embraced everything from disco through rap, rock, jazz and blues.

The "Queen West scene" used to be exactly that — on Queen Street. But like any good idea whose time has arrived, it was difficult to contain. The spread was to the south. Warehouses once filled with office furniture, dry goods, and machine parts, and factory buildings where row upon row of sewing machine operators turned out the latest in fashions now harbour upscale restaurants and bars. The parallel section on King W. will round out your options in this part of town.

You say you want to be on TV? For a loonie (Canada's dollar coin) you can hop into the street-side booth at Queen and John, tell it all to a TV camera, then watch it later on CITY TV's Speaker's Corner show.

Highlights

401 RICHMOND LIMITED (401 Richmond W., 595-5900). On the outside of this converted warehouse, huge fabric banners depicting artisans at work give the passer-by a sense of what's happening inside. The most important features of 401 Richmond are the living, breathing kind. 401 Richmond is home to more than 130 artists, activists and entrepreneurs whose ideas, art works, products and services reflect Toronto's most innovative and creative edge.

There's always something exciting happening in the galleries and workshops. Check out A-Space, YYZ and Gallery 4. Go on in, grab a fair trade coffee at the Loftus Lloyd Café or savour a salad with herbs from the roof garden. Behind the 401 building in the coachhouse you'll also find Cinecycle (971-4273), an underground 35mm cinema and bike repair shop.

SIR WILLIAM CAMPBELL HOUSE (160 Queen W. at University, 597-0227). If you've ever wondered what life was like for the well-to-do of colonial times, this 1820s home of the Chief Justice of Upper Canada and his family is the museum for you. Take a cooking class in a period kitchen. Tour with guides who wear period clothing. Enjoy the traditional gardens. Campbell House did not start out here. It was originally in the Old Town near Adelaide and Frederick Sts. In 1972, to make way for development and to avoid demolition, it was hoisted onto the back of a truck and moved to its present location. So precariously was it balanced on a 56 wheel flatbed that the truck was simply moved ahead a few feet at a time, and then the house was winched slowly forward. It took 6 hours to move about one and a half kilometres (about 1 mile). Adults $3.50, seniors/students $2.50, children $2.

Things to Do, See, Buy & Eat

THE REX HOTEL (194 Queen W., 598-2475). This is where musicians come to hear jazz.
URBANE CYCLIST (180 John, 979-9733). Bicycles, repairs and great accessories.
THE ORGANIC FARMERS MARKET (238 Queen W., near McCaul Ave., 422-1944). Saturday 8 to 2 year-round.
THE ORGANIC FARMERS MARKET OUTLET & FARM KITCHEN (238 Queen W., near McCaul Ave.). In the 1830's, the farmer who bequeathed the property to the city stipulated that it always be used by the community for food service. The organic food store is open seven days a week.
THE BODY SHOP (286 Queen W., 599-4385). Cosmetics and body care that also cares for the environment. Many locations throughout Toronto.
BLACK BULL HOTEL AND TAVERN (298 Queen W., 593-2766). A great place to warm up and slurp a beer in winter. In summer, you can sit on the patio beside row upon row of motorcycles and watch the passing parade with the jolly bikers.
CITY TV (299 Queen W., 591-5757). Press your face up against the Queen window of the live broadcast studio and hope the camera pans your way. Spend a loonie at Speaker's Corner to have your say.
JUICE FOR LIFE (336 Queen W., 599-4442). Gourmet juice bar and vegan restaurant - they also give compost away to local residents who request it for their gardens.
LUSH (312 Queen W., 599-5874). All natural bath and beauty products (most products are vegan friendly).
GWENDOLYNE HATS (401 Richmond W., 351-1219). One-of-a-kind hats designed and created by artists and sold on the premises.

FRESSEN RESTAURANT (478 Queen W., 504-5127). Herbivorous cuisine for an array of tastes.
BUTLER'S PANTRY CAFÉ (482–484 Queen W., 504-3414). Great weekend brunch.

Queen Street West West

Queen between Bathurst and Dovercourt.

Don't stop too soon, if you continue west, you'll run across a hip little stretch of Queen filled with antique stores, used bookstores, cafés, local fashion designers, art and photo galleries, a music gallery and vintage clothing stores. Don't miss it!

Things to Do, See, Buy & Eat

AZUL RESTAURANT (181 Bathurst, 703-9360). Organic food and great patio.
STEPHEN BULGER GALLERY (700 Queen W., 504-0575). Gallery specializing in Canadian and international photography.
ALEX WILSON COMMUNITY GARDEN (552 Richmond W). The garden has a boardwalk that connects Richmond to Queen. Alex Wilson was one of Toronto's earliest garden activists/enthusiasts and after his death, this community garden was dedicated to his memory.
APPLETREE NATURAL FOODS (752 Queen W., 504-9677). Organic veggies and take-out lunch stand.
GYPSY CO-OP (817 Queen W., 703-5069). Beanery, candy store, tarot readings and great food too.
JAPANESE PAPER PLACE (887 Queen W., 703-0089). A supply store for artists, it's a great place to buy hand-crafted items made from paper from around the world.
THE SWAN RESTAURANT (892 Queen W., 532-0452). Exquisite food and an exclusive wine list (they often have organic wines available) in a restored diner setting.
XXX DINER (894 Queen W., 536-2822). Known as the "Triple-X" this brunch spot on the edge of Trinity-Bellwoods Park is popular with artists and film industry types.
BACCHUS ROTI (1376 Queen W.,way west, 532-8191). Caribbean cuisine using fresh produce for fillings in these tasty wraps/rotis.
NINE OF CUPS RESTAURANT (1522 Queen W., way west., 532-2216). Informal, friendly and occasional starting point for "Haunted Parkdale" tours.
SWALLOW (1544 Queen W., way west, 535-1811). Its backyard patio doubles as an organic garden.

EASY (1645 Queen W., way west). One of the area's hip cafés with a good Sunday brunch (also only a 15-minute walk to High Park, Bloor and Keele).

Queen Street — Heading East

Queen East near Yonge is the perfect place for an intensive half-day of touring. Just south of Dundas on Yonge are two of Toronto's finest theatres. The Pantages has been a vaudeville house, motion picture palace and a cinema multiplex. Now it's back to live top-of-the-line theatre. Down the street, the Elgin & Winter Garden, a two-storey theatre-cum-movie house, has returned to its former glory as a live venue.

Behind the theatres is Massey Hall, at Shuter and Victoria Sts. Built in 1892 as Toronto's premiere concert venue, it is still in use. As a Designated Heritage Structure, it should be around for years to come.

Heading east, you pass St. Michael's Hospital. To its north, up Church is St. Michael's Roman Catholic Cathedral. Built in 1841, it's worth a look for its sumptuous interior and stained glass windows. Besides the Cathedral, you can visit **Mackenzie House** Museum (see below). Across from the Cathedral on Church is pawn shop row where an interesting hour can be spent just looking over the incredible selection of stuff people have brought in.

Cross Jarvis at Queen and look for a compact couple of block's worth of antique and speciality shops. Furniture, clothing, jewellery and bric-a-brac of every description, new, used, or somewhere in between — is all here.

From here you can take a 10-minute streetcar ride east along Queen to the Riverdale neighbourhood, or head farther east for about half an hour to The Beaches (see page 16).

Highlights

MACKENZIE HOUSE (82 Bond at Church, 392-6915). In 1837, unhappy with the political direction the country was taking, William Lyon Mackenzie orchestrated an unsuccessful attempt to overthrow the government of Upper Canada.

For this he was exiled for 12 years before receiving a pardon. He lived in this house from 1859 to 1861. It has been fully restored and has a working printing press like the one Mackenzie would have used for his newspaper, *The Colonial Advocate*. Tours and demonstrations are available. Adults $3.50, seniors/students $2.75, children $2.50.

Things to Do, See, Buy & Eat

ELGIN & WINTER GARDEN THEATRE CENTRE (189 Yonge, 314-2901). A national historic site, this theatre is the last "double-decker"/stacked Edwardian theatre operating in the world. Tours available.

MASSEY HALL (178 Victoria, 872-4255). Concert goers will enjoy this 2,800-seat acoustic gem.

PANTAGES THEATRE (244 Victoria, 364-4100). This historic 2,200-seat theatre is supposedly haunted.

Riverdale

The Essence

To see all of Riverdale, you will need more than one day, and you will have to cover all the ground bounded by Broadview in the west, Danforth in the north, Greenwood in the east and Lake Ontario to the south. If you're looking for shady streets where you can take a summer walk or relaxing parks where you can pause and reflect, you'll find them. But there's another, edgier side to Riverdale as well.

Simmering just below the serenity is a strong activist character. Whether it's because of deep working class roots, or an independent spirit that survived the early twentieth century bridging of the Don Valley, you know Riverdale will not be tread on. When a waterfront incinerator was determined to be a health hazard to Riverdale, the response was swift and emphatic. Community groups sprang up and launched discussions with the City that resulted in the end of incineration.

When the Don River became so polluted that it threatened the health of anyone who approached it, action groups formed, many having Riverdale roots. Today, community centres and advocacy groups abound and address the whole gamut of health, social and economic issues, making Riverdale one of Toronto's most socially conscious communities.

Riverdale is also one of Toronto's most highly liveable neighbourhoods. Most Riverdale homes were built between 1880 and 1924, giving the place that lived-in feeling. Overall, Riverdale is quiet, with large maples lining the streets. Along its northern and southern boundaries, it really bustles, influenced by the bistros and shops of Greektown on the Danforth and by the relentless traffic along Queen East. Plenty of open space complements the trendy businesses that are reclaiming the old industrial neighbourhoods.

Queen-Broadview Village is the oldest part of Riverdale. It is rich in local history, antique and collectible stores, and a growing number of studios and galleries. A stairway provides Queen street access to the Lower Don Trail where you can walk, run, in-line skate or cycle. Farther north at Gerrard and Broadview is a smaller, later version of downtown's Chinatown. Beyond that is Riverdale Park (see page 66).

At the south eastern end of things is a funky little neighbourhood of artists, photographers, graphic designers, cinematographers and producers. Industrial buildings and warehouses are now lofts, film studios and production houses. Known as Leslieville and the Studio District, this little point of light is situated along Queen E. between Logan and Connaught and along Carlaw.

The *Healthy House,* a private residence in Toronto, was developed to provide an example of renewable energy resources, energy efficiency, wastewater management and sustainable design. With no municipal, gas or water connections, the house is fully independent from municipal services. [9]

The Roots — A Taste of History

In the late 1700s, John Scadding was granted the lands that include Riverdale. It remained a small rural community until the Grand Trunk Railway came through in the mid-1850s. New industry and resulting employment opportunities attracted labourers, some of whom settled here and built the area's first homes in the southern extreme. Riverdale remained largely undeveloped north of Queen until 1884.

Even then, Riverdale could only be reached from Toronto by dipping through the Don Valley at Queen and then heading north up Broadview. Poor roads, marshy terrain and anything but the best of weather made the trip unwelcome to say the least. The 1918 construction of Toronto's largest bridge, the Prince Edward Viaduct (see page 101) forged a link at the north end of Riverdale to the City of Toronto across the Don River. This new ease of access opened a floodgate. Builders, home buyers and businesses surged through, marking the turning point in the emergence of the Riverdale community.

Highlights

RIVERDALE PARK (Broadview and Gerrard E., 392-1111). The land for Riverdale Park was purchased by the City of Toronto in 1856. It is divided in two by the Don River and the Don Valley expressway.

It's easy to stroll from Cabbagetown's streets lined with trees and Victorian houses (one of the largest concentrations in Canada) to the Danforth. Just cut through Riverdale Farm, across the bridge, and across the running field, past the tennis courts up to Danforth. While visiting the park be sure to see Riverdale Farm (see page 76).

DON JAIL / TORONTO JAIL (550 Gerrard E). Take a stroll past — the building strikes awe if the sun is shining and the sky is blue. The Don Jail opened for business in 1864 and served Toronto for 113 years. Its design and planning reflected Victorian ideas of justice.

Influenced by John Howard's principals of "security, reform, and, salubrity" (that is, a clean, healthy and wholesome environment), the jail was abutted by an industrial farm and a house of refuge (an interesting term for poor house). To ensure security, the jail was built at what was then some distance from town. It overlooked the clean, healthy and wholesome Don Valley. Hard work and instructional programs at the industrial farm encouraged reform.

Things to Do, See, Buy & Eat

SEPHIROTH (898 Queen E., 461-4612). Health food store and juice bar.

BROKEN FENCE SOCIETY (63 Broadview, Suite 413, 469-0153, call first). Environmental art, newsletters and exhibits.

RIVERDALE BRANCH PUBLIC LIBRARY (370 Broadview, 393-7720). The library, which dates from 1910, was one of the first public libraries built in Toronto. Funding was donated by the Andrew Carnegie Foundation in a program through which they endowed libraries in Canada and the United States.

RIVERDALE COMMUNITY BUSINESS CENTRE (1007 Gerrard E., 462-0496, www.riverdale.org). Self-guided heritage walks that include interesting sites like Degrassi (where the Degrassi TV series was filmed), the Opera House (Toronto's longest operating live music theatre), Toronto Groceterias (almost unchanged since 1885) and more.

SHAKESPEARE IN THE ROUGH
(www.shakesintherough.com). Fully professional theatre company playing at Withrow Park, (McConnell and Logan Ave). on Fridays, Saturdays, Sundays and public holidays from July through Labour Day weekend. Pay-what-you-can.

Dundas Street — Heading West

Like all of our other major downtown streets, Dundas can change costume in a flash. A few streetcar stops slip by and you think you've changed cities. Standing between Queen and College, it is influenced by the best of both. A good idea on Queen might have a major influence on everything for blocks around, including Dundas. Similarly things that percolate down from College hit Dundas hard.

Planning an itinerary means considering all members of the triumvirate as they make their way across town.

The average visitor to Toronto returns an average of 17 times. 10

Chinatown

Dundas from Bay to Spadina, north on Spadina to College.

The Essence

A trip to Chinatown is almost like a visit to the Far East. On a busy day, as you make your way through and around the bustling crowds and merchants' sidewalk stalls, you are immersed in the look, feel, smells and tastes of Asia (see Photo section). Toronto has the largest Asian population in North America. Almost one-third live in this area - and many more come to work here. There are actually two downtown Chinatown areas, the other one is to the east at Broadview and Gerrard E. in Riverdale (see page 64).

Shopping in Chinatown is a great adventure. Start with fresh fruit and vegetables (some of which you may never have seen before and have absolutely no idea how to prepare). Move on to quirky bargain shops with everything from computers to the latest styles in sunglasses, all on sale at a price that is, more often than not, negotiable.

Then again, you could concentrate on the restaurants. They are everywhere. Choices run the gamut from modest cafeteria-style barbecue-and-noodle shops to intimate, Asian-style fine dining. And the menu will let you be as adventurous as you dare. With a little guidance from your server, you can try some very exotic cuisine.

Of course, when you've shopped, and your stomach is full, experience the festivities. For example, during Chinese New Year, the streets light up with the Lantern Festival when jesters swinging colourful lanterns provoke a grimacing dragon or lion as it undulates through the streets while the bang of firecrackers drives away evil spirits.

Chinatown

The Roots — A Taste of History

Chinese immigrants were lured to Canada by the promise of easy riches in the western gold rushes, and, later, to toil as labourers building the Canadian Pacific Railway. Those who made their way to Toronto settled in the York area around today's City Hall. They opened hand laundries, small tea shops, vegetable stalls, and restaurants. A newspaper and a church soon followed.

In the 1950s, much of the original Chinatown was razed to make way for Toronto's new City Hall. Relocated towards Dundas and Spadina the community continues to flourish and to grow.

Highlights

ART GALLERY OF ONTARIO (AGO) / THE GRANGE HISTORIC HOUSE (317 Dundas W., 979-6608). The AGO has a fine selection of international and Canadian works, including the Group of Seven. It also holds the world's largest public collection of works by British sculptor Henry Moore.

The first art gallery opened in 1900 on the site of the current AGO. The Art Museum of Toronto was housed in an 1817 home known as the Grange (now incorporated into the gallery itself). It is one of the four oldest buildings in Toronto and is fully restored. A real treat is the working kitchen, where you can enjoy samples of cuisine that might have been prepared for the original owners and their guests.

Eat in the peaceful atrium restaurant overlooking the gardens or enjoy a picnic in Grange Park, south of the Art Gallery, a lovely retreat. General admission for the AGO is "pay-what-you-can" (suggested $6). Admission fees apply to special exhibits.

BALDWIN STREET EAST (One block north of Dundas, west of McCaul). This short stretch of street is a lively, unintentional secret in Toronto. Walking west along Baldwin from McCaul for about a block you can experience the ambience of an artist's colony in the heart of town. Health food stores, vegetarian restaurants and cafés, shops selling everything from vintage records to Chinese pastries line this neighbourhood.

LIVING WALL: CANADA LIFE ASSURANCE BUILDING (180 Simcoe, behind 330 University, 597-1440). In an interesting experiment, plants are being used to clean the air. The plants form a "breathing wall" that is a tropical ecosystem in miniature, built into a conference room as its sole air conditioning system. The breathing wall is so successful in the conference room that Canada Life hopes to hook it into the air circulation system for the first three floors of the building.

Things to Do, See, Buy & Eat

DELTA CHELSEA (33 Gerrard W., 595-1975). This hotel is working on its green initiatives. Check out the courtyard dining, an inner-city green oasis.

LE COMMENSAL FINE VEGETARIAN CUISINE (655 Bay, 596-9364). A wonderful vegetarian salad bar, where food is sold by weight.

MAX TANNENBAUM GARDEN (16th Fl., Princess Margaret Hospital, 610 University). Open to public. Closed in winter. Outside perennial garden provides a quiet retreat.

MUSEUM FOR TEXTILES (55 Centre, University and Dundas, 599-5321). The only museum devoted to collection of contemporary and traditional textiles from all over the world. Exhibits and classes are continually changing (see page 173).

THE GRANGE (317 Dundas W., 979-6608). Offers entertaining, experiential history lessons for youngsters 8-12 through games, tours, and baking. Grange Park, south of the Art Gallery, is great for picnics.

CINEMATHÈQUE REPERTORY CINEMA JACKMAN HALL (Art Gallery of Ontario, 317 Dundas W., 968-3456). Shows a selection of Canadian, foreign and arthouse films including timeless classics and rarely-seen restored prints. Fully wheelchair accessible.

LOTUS GARDEN (393 Dundas W., 598-1883). Buddhist vegetarian cooking. Try their organic durian shakes.

YUNG SING PASTRY SHOP (22 Baldwin, 979-2832). The oldest family-run Chinese bakery in Toronto. Formerly a Kosher butcher shop. You can get lunch for under $5.

GROSSMAN'S TAVERN (379 Spadina, 977-7000). A Toronto landmark pub. Over the years, a home to artists, musicians, poets, professors, draft dodgers and, well, just about anyone.

CO YEN (334 Spadina, 597-1573). Great vegetarian spring rolls.

MANDARIN THEATRE (287 Spadina). Built in 1921 as a Yiddish theatre, it operated as a movie house, and later a burlesque theatre, and then a Chinese-language movie house in 1980. It is now a gift shop.

SUPER SPROUTS (205 Spadina, 977-7796). An indoor organic sprout farm with over 25 kinds of sprouts, and a resource centre on diet, vegetarianism, organics, and raw foods.

Visitor Information

TRAVELLERS AID SOCIETY OF TORONTO
Toronto Coach Terminal (see page 18).

Kensington Market

Between Baldwin, Kensington, Dundas and Augusta.

The Essence

Kensington Market is about everything that signifies neighbourhood. Day and night, life here is a lusty affair, international in spirit, with the colours, sounds and foods of Europe, Africa, Asia, the Caribbean and South America. Each newly-arrived immigrant group firmly believed that they could find everything they needed close to home, at reasonable prices, seven days a week, from local independent shopkeepers. In Kensington Market they made it happen. The open-air market offers exotic foods, designer clothing, handmade crafts and gifts and jewellery from around the world.

More than 170 different languages are spoken in Toronto and you'll hear them all down here. Music makes night seem eternal in the mysterious heart of Kensington Market. Bars and bistros bring together music makers of every stripe.

Kensington Market

The Roots — A Taste of History

In its first incarnation, this densely forested area was where native peoples met to fish, trade and live beside the many streams and creeks now hidden beneath the city.

The first Europeans in Toronto were given 40.5 hectare (100 acre) lots in 1793 as an inducement to stay. With the arrival of poor English and Irish settlers, the land was sliced up to provide for modest housing. Soon the new arrivals had forged local business opportunities in a community they could call their own. Even after 200 years, this is still the starting point for many of the city's newcomers.

European Jews gave way to the Italians and Ukrainians, who were in turn displaced by new arrivals from Portugal, Hungary, the Caribbean and Hong Kong. By 1960, the Portuguese exerted the major influence.

In the mid-1960s, an urban renewal program called for the demolition of old buildings in favour of new. Market dwellers united in revolt and were successful in gaining a say in the future of their neighbourhood. Residents and city dwellers worked together in a spirit of compromise.

The residents won some battles (canopies over the sidewalks stayed), but lost others (live chickens went).

Moving into the 1970s, Chinatown sprang up around Kensington, adding yet another dimension to the complex texture of the market.

There will always be new arrivals to put their stamp on the market. They may be upscale condo dwellers, or struggling immigrants, but the spirit of Kensington will overtake them as it has in generations past; they will forge an island of close community in a sea of big city reserve.

Things to Do, See, Buy & Eat

52 INC. (394 College, 906-0334). A hip alternative cafe / gallery serving fair trade coffee. It also often hosts benefits.

OK HEALTH VEGETARIAN RESTAURANT LTD. (256 Augusta, 971-9067). Not only is it vegetarian, it also maintains ecofriendly business operations. Won the healthy lifestyle award for Chinatown's cleanest kitchen and washrooms.

EZA WEAR (256D Augusta, 975-1388). Clothing and more housed in a store made of recycled materials; also a little gallery space that showcases local artists.

ST. STEPHEN-IN-THE-FIELDS ANGLICAN CHURCH (103 Bellevue). A Heritage Site, this church was rebuilt after a fire in 1865, and in March 1927 pioneered regular church service radio broadcasting.

KENSINGTON FIRE HALL (NO. 8 STATION) (132 Bellevue). Built in 1878, it housed the city's first motorized fire engine. As part of a neighbourhood tradition, the hall's bell is rung every night at 9.

MY MARKET BAKERY (172 Baldwin, 593-6772). Sister store to Cheese Magic, this bakery sells ginormous ginger and oatmeal cookies for $1.

CHEESE MAGIC (182 Baldwin, 593-9531). The market's favorite cheese store also sells fresh ground peanut butter, smoked salmon and homemade hummous.

MOONBEAM CAFÉ (30 Andrew, 595-0327). Fair trade coffee, organic home roasted beans and great vegetarian food. Recycled coffee bean bags are used as seat covers.

BRIGHT PEARL SEAFOOD RESTAURANT (346-348 Spadina, 979-3988). Great seafood menu.

PRESERVING OUR HEALTH COMMUNITY GARDEN (707 Dundas W., behind Scadding Court Community Centre, 392-1668). This garden was created by local parents and includes an herb garden, a greenhouse, a worm composting project and a children's program.

Roncesvalles

The Essence

Roncesvalles is the continuation of Dundas heading south of Boustead.

If you're looking for great deli, jerk chicken, a falafel, or fresh baked Italian bread, it's all here within a few short blocks. Then if you want to wash it all down with a good old Canadian style beer and a pickled egg, you can. This is a truly eclectic neighbourhood with all the charm of a small community.

Roncesvalles from the Lakeshore to Dundas West is also known as Little Poland. Savour a taste of this culture in the many Polish bakeries and shops. There are also funky little neighbourhood coffee shops that often display local art on their walls. At its southern end, where it merges with King and Queen W., an impressive now fully-ramped pedestrian bridge spans Lakeshore allowing safe passage to the lakefront and the Palais Royale Ballroom.

Highlights

PALAIS ROYALE BALLROOM (1601 Lake Shore Blvd. W). If you like to dance, to really "cut a rug", you should see this Toronto original - one of the earliest and best sprung wooden dance floors ever built. The ballroom is currently closed due to fire damage, but after being refurbished, it is slated to re-open as a prime lakefront dance venue. It has quite a history, having played host to Woody Herman, Tommy and Jimmy Dorsey, Bob Crosby, Bert Niosi, Glen Miller, Harry James, Charlie Barnett, Duke Ellington, Count Basie, Benny Goodman, Sammy Kaye and more. The Historical Board tells us that the Palais Royale "opened in 1922 as both a dance hall and Walter Dean's Boat Factory. Remodelled in 1924 and 1928, it housed various nightclubs and restaurants and became one of the most famous of Toronto's dance halls".

Things to Do, See, Buy & Eat

MITZI'S CAFÉ AND GALLERY (100 Sorauren, 588-1234). Great brunch spot!

HELEN'S NATURAL FOODS (283 Roncesvalles, 534-1833). Natural and bulk food, organic produce, magazines and health products.

ALTERNATIVE GROUNDS COFFEEHOUSE & ROASTERY (333 Roncesvalles, 534-5543). Organic and fair-trade coffee, great community atmosphere and place for kids to play with toys and books.

REVUE REPERTORY CINEMA (400 Roncesvalles, 531-9959). Wheelchair accessible.

GATE 403 RESTAURANT AND BAR (403 Roncesvalles, 588-2930). Great jazz and dinner club.

RIVER CAFÉ (413 Roncesvalles, 535-3422). Eclectic food and atmosphere and wood shop business.

The Junction

The Essence and Roots

The Junction is an area bounded by Dundas, Bloor, St Clair W. and Runnymede. The community dates back to the 1880's and the arrival of the Grand Trunk, Toronto Grey and Bruce, and Northern railway lines. Industry soon followed, along with workers from many lands who chose to set down roots here.

The Junction thrived as an industrial satellite of Toronto and for over a quarter of a century was a separate municipality. Over time and with the decline of industrial activity in the area, affordable housing and converted warehouse space adapted for working studios have attracted the artists, musicians, and kindred spirits who so thoroughly animate this neighbourhood.

Closer to Bloor, it has much in common with the High Park neighbourhood it abuts. Tree-lined streets and wide front lawns make this a great strolling site. Major revitalization efforts are underway on the Dundas West commercial strip, which offers an eclectic mix of storefronts of architectural distinction.

Dundas Street — Heading East

One block north of Dundas and Yonge on Gould is Chess Game Corner. No matter what the weather, you can see chess players setting up their timers and squaring off for some intense play. A block east at Gould and Victoria is the Ryerson skating rink ornamented with rocks from northern Ontario. While you're there, walk in the quadrangle oasis that is the Ryerson University campus. A ten-minute streetcar ride east along Dundas brings you to the southern tip of Cabbagetown and, if you wish, you can continue on just across the Don Valley into Riverdale (see page 64.)

Cabbagetown

The Essence

Cabbagetown folks take great pride in their end of town. It is one of Toronto's most popular neighbourhoods. The arts thrive here, there's great dining, great heritage architecture, and the community's multicultural make-up gives it a worldly-wise flavour.

Official Cabbagetown boundaries are Wellesley E., Parliament, the Don Valley, and Gerrard. To capitalize on the prized Cabbagetown cachet anyone living east of Parliament from Bloor to Queen might refer to their neighbourhood as Cabbagetown. In any event, you can comfortably explore the original Cabbagetown in a day of dedicated walking and browsing.

The Centre for Social Justice builds partnerships with various social movements to promote equality and economic and social justice. Visit www.socialjustice.com for more info.

The Roots — A Taste of History

In the early 19th century, most of Cabbagetown's lands were designated as a government reserve. Cleared for much-needed lumber, it was then to accommodate a naval shipyard. For a variety of reasons, this didn't happen. By 1819 the land had been subdivided for housing lots. Popular opinion held that the mainly dank, marshy land was unhealthy. People moved west instead.

By 1840, Irish immigrants arrived, escaping from the potato famines at home. With little money, their choices were limited and despite concerns about the unhealthy conditions, they moved in. To survive grinding poverty, many took to planting front-yard market gardens. The most commonly planted item was cabbage. Cabbagetown emerged as a poor but spirited neighbourhood of working-class homes and corner shops.

Through the 1870s and 80s, an immigration spurt created a land crisis. Suddenly, Cabbagetown was a popular place. You could get land cheap and build an elegant, imposing house from which to survey the gentle rise north toward the cemetery, the westward rolling hills of the Don Valley, and the view south to the lake.

Always struggling to survive, the more marginal Cabbagetown residents were driven to new depths by the Great Depression of the 1930s. At its lowest ebb, novelist

Hugh Garner, a native and chronicler of Cabbagetown, wrote that the Depression made of Cabbagetown the most desperate Anglo Saxon slum on the continent.

Cabbagetown came back to life in the 1970s and 1980s. Property ownership was fast moving out of the financial reach of most people. But, you could still get a deal in Cabbagetown. Many recent buyers restored their purchases to former Victorian splendour. Cabbagetown is now considered one of Toronto's most gentrified neighbourhoods.

Highlights

RIVERDALE FARM (201 Winchester and Sumach, 392-6794). Find out how to milk a cow, separate cream, and make butter. Learn about sheep shearing, wool spinning and dying, and floral and herb gardening. Help collect eggs. Enjoy a visit with the horses, cows, pigs, goats, chickens and rare breeds of early Ontario livestock the farm is raising to prevent their species from dying out. Self-guided tours are supported by knowledgeable on-site farm attendants.

The Farm is open 365 days a year and farm hours change with the seasons (see Photo section).

WINCHESTER HOTEL (531 Parliament, 929-1875). For a hard driving, hard drinking, rhythm-n-blues and rock-n-roll night out, try the Winchester.

JAMES L. MORRISON HOUSE (37 Metcalfe). The initial impression is that you are looking at a yard sale for Victorian mouldings or a billboard ad for Classical Revival. In fact, the explanation for this house is simple but weird. It was built to face north across a broad expanse of land onto Winchester. Its front and side were given the full treatment in respect of decoration. A later owner sold the land between the house and Winchester, leaving it with a new frontage on Metcalfe. When an apartment building was erected on the Winchester side, the house's owner, not wanting to waste the elaborate mouldings on the north side of the house which now faced a brick wall, moved them to the Metcalfe side, leaving it, to some minds, a tad overdone. The inside is not accessible to the public but makes a memorable walk-by.

ALLAN GARDENS (19 Horticultural, near Sherbourne and Carlton, 392-7288). Even if you don't know a dandelion from an aspidistra, you will still be glad you came to Allan Gardens (see Photo section). Winter or summer, it's a guaranteed escape from the world outside with 1440 square metres (16,000 square feet) of greenhouse holding tropical and subtropical plants. Climate-controlled rooms in the 90-year-old historical Palm House maintain environments that support tropical plants in one wing and desert cacti in another.

Pandanus (Madagascar tropical pine), orchids, various hibiscus, bromeliads and cacti, caladiums and amaryllis make the garden a favourite choice for bridal photos and park concerts.

The park and garden date from 1858 when prominent local figure George William Allan donated a 2 hectare (5 acre) oval of land to the Toronto Horticultural Society. In ensuing years, the park was turned over to the City of Toronto and supplemented by additional lands and it now occupies almost an entire city block. The building standing today dates from 1909 and has recently undergone sensitive renovation.

Things to Do, See, Buy & Eat

RESTAURANTS. If you're thinking of eating and people watching, it's hard to go wrong in Cabbagetown during the warmer months. Almost all the restaurants and bars in this neighbourhood have patios. But year-round there's always ample choice — just have a wander.

LENNIE'S (489 Parliament, 920-3777). Natural foods, also some organics, and homeopathic and other vitamins and supplements.

THE JET FUEL (519 Parliament, 968-9982). A popular (great coffee) hangout for artists, bike couriers and other bohemian types.

DANIEL ET DANIEL CATERING (248 Carlton, 968-9275). Good coffee and great pastries.

TORONTO NECROPOLIS AND CREMATORIUM (200 Winchester, 928-7911). Extravagant grounds and stunning porte cochère and lodge (circa 1850) across from Riverdale Farm.

Gerrard — India Bazaar

A promenade through a section of Gerrard E. between Greenwood and Coxwell presents you with the shops of the Gerrard India Bazaar, one of the largest markets of its kind in North America. This short section of street and shops offers anything from exquisite saris and magnificent textiles to books and tapes of various Indian cultures (available at news agents and the local library). Weekends and evenings, the neighbourhood comes alive as people old and young enjoy the lively atmosphere.

To get a real feel for this east end jewel, spend an afternoon or evening shopping at one of the many jewellery or clothing stores and dining on exotic food at a local restaurant. Then, take in an East Indian film at the Gerrard Street Cinema, or an event at the Indian Centre. Exciting annual events like the Baisakhi (Spring) Festival, fall's Diwali (Festival of Lights) and the Eid (Ramadan) celebration give added atmosphere to this bustling community.

College Street — Heading West

College is the third member of the group of streets that define downtown. Heading west, it touches the University of Toronto. Farther on, you move into Little Italy. For all things Italian, come here. You'll also experience a bit of Latin American influence — Brazilian, Peruvian and more. To the north lies a sister neighbourhood, Corso Italia (not to be confused with Little Italy), launched when folks from down here felt the need branch out. It too has the real taste of Italy. (See page 142.)

Toronto has the largest Italian population outside of Italy. [11]

University of Toronto (U of T)

The Essence

U of T reaches east and west from Bay to Spadina and from Bloor in the north to College at its southern end. It is a long walk around this campus (all 64 hectares / 160 acres!), but it's definitely worth it.

You'll see old buildings and new — many covered in ivy — with beautifully manicured lawns and gardens. Lecture halls, theatres, historic buildings and all the social amenities of campus life are found here. U of T has 19 separate centres that work on environmental issues related to ecology, social issues, economics and other disciplines. William Lyon Mackenzie King (Canada's tenth Prime Minister), Adrienne Clarkson (Canada's current Governor-General), artist William Hutt and author Margaret Atwood all graduated from here. It's impossible here to detail all that is on offer at U of T. For a closer look, it's best to call the main number (978-5000) and ask about tours, current events, and more.

The Roots — A Taste of History

The University of Toronto dates back to 1827, when a

royal charter was obtained for King's College by Upper Canada's Anglican elite. It was the colony's first institution of higher learning. This spanking-new university, controlled by the Church of England, opened for business in 1843. King's College was then secularised by the provincial government in 1849 and renamed the University of Toronto. Various religious groups, feeling that an education without their input was inadequate, responded by opening their own colleges and universities, which were ultimately absorbed into U of T over time.

The most familiar of the university buildings, University College, has a ghost story to tell. At the west side of the main building and off the covered walkway is a large solid door marred by two unmistakable gashes.

The story goes that two masons involved in the original construction came to grief over the love of a woman. On a presumably dark and stormy night, one of the swains took up an axe and pursued the other, swinging as he ran. The blows that missed took chunks out of the door. The body was never recovered, but according to legend, the ghost still walks.

On only a slightly less ghostly note, Hart House, opened as a leisure faculty for men, did not admit women until 1972. Today a Canadiana art collection is housed here.

Visitor Information

NONA MCDONALD VISITOR CENTRE (FOR U OF T) (25 King's College Circle, University of Toronto, 978-5000). Free campus tours available Monday to Friday.

UNIVERSITY OF TORONTO OPERATOR (978-2011). General contact information.

Highlights

TADDLE CREEK. Now flowing under the U of T campus, Taddle Creek was once one of Toronto's major waterways. You can get an idea of its course by just strolling down Philosopher's Walk from Bloor just behind the Royal Ontario Museum. The path follows the course of the creek down to College Street.

The first Parliament buildings for Upper Canada were located near the mouth of Taddle Creek and it ran through many prominent early Torontonian estates. With no sewage infrastructure at the time, people used the creek to carry untreated sanitary sewage away directly into Toronto Bay. This became a major health issue. By 1881, contamination had gotten out of control and so the last visible section of

Taddle Creek was finally buried in 1884.

Taddle Creek also interfered with the development of a surface transportation system that would follow a planned grid pattern. So with increasing development, the creek's life tributaries were re-routed, buried, drained or just stopped up. In time it became less of an impediment as its flow diminished. But Taddle Creek gets even. Basement flooding is still common for many buildings standing above its course.

There is sincere interest in the restoration not only of Taddle Creek, but also of many buried water courses throughout the city. Taddle Creek waits underground while concerned people in various ecological groups and organizations strive to preserve and restore the natural landscape and waterscape of Toronto (see Resource Groups page 151).

ROYAL ONTARIO MUSEUM (ROM) (100 Queen's Park Cres. at Bloor W., 586-8000, not far from U of T). Stop over in a bat cave, a tropical forest or a biodiversity gallery. Get up close and personal with an Egyptian mummy, a medieval knight or a big batch of bugs. Visit world famous Chinese and Canadiana Collections. The ROM is a compelling and informative place to spend time. Canada's largest museum holds a universe within its walls and offers free guided walking tours daily. The only disappointment might be that your feet will give out before your interest does. A thorough investigation here could take days. Special exhibits and events vary throughout the year. Adults $12, seniors/students $8, children $6, children under 4 get in free.

THE CHILDREN'S OWN MUSEUM (COM) (90 Queen's Park Cres., 542-1492).The Children's Own Museum is in the former planetarium building at the south end of the ROM. It offers great hands-on and facilitated play-based learning for young children ages one to eight years old and is designed to stimulate their thinking, imagination and personal growth. General admission is $4.75, children under one get in free.

GEORGE R. GARDINER MUSEUM OF CERAMIC ART (111 Queens Park Cres., south of Bloor, 586-8080). Devoted to ceramics and ceramic research, this museum was founded in 1984 by George R. Gardiner and his wife Helen to house their international collection of ceramics from Europe, Asia and the Americas. It now houses more than 2,600 ceramic works. Special programmes include decorative arts lectures by international scholars as well as identification clinics.

The Museum Shop specializes in contemporary Canadian ceramics and features the work of a different Canadian artist each month. You may also choose to lunch at the museum's restaurant, or take an afternoon tea. Adults $10, seniors / students / children $6. First Tuesday of each month admission is free.

There are 374 bird species of wild occurrence within a 50km radius of the ROM. [12]

Things to Do, See, Buy & Eat

HURON ST. COMMUNITY GARDEN (239 College, behind Lillian H. Smith Library, 392-1668). One of the first of Toronto's 'new' community gardens, this one shows us that a vegetable garden can exist in a public park, can be beautiful, and doesn't have to be rectangular.

UNIVERSITY OF TORONTO. Call 978-5000 for locations.

KING'S COLLEGE CIRCLE. A wonderful vantage point for seeing some of the main university buildings and getting a feel of the campus.

UNIVERSITY COLLEGE. Crops up frequently in movies as a castle, a mansion, and, occasionally, a university.

MEDICAL SCIENCES BUILDING. Has a large modern theatre fully equipped to screen cinemascope movies, and many showings are free.

CONVOCATION HALL. A vast auditorium also used for an occasional rock concert, it has a breathtaking interior.

PARLIAMENT BUILDING OF ONTARIO (QUEEN'S PARK) (Queen's Park Circle, 325-7500 for tours). The seat of parliament in Ontario is imposingly placed at the top of University Avenue. Local protests and demonstrations often happen on its doorstep. The park behind is a great place to run, rest, relax and eat lunch.

ARCHIVES OF ONTARIO (77 Grenville, Suite 300, 327-1600). Abundant material and images about the history and government of Ontario dating back as far as 1720, including oral history tapes, cartographic, architectural and photographic materials.

BILL DUNPHY MEMORIAL COMMUNITY GARDEN (43 Queen's Park Circle, 392-1668). This garden presents an edible landscape that includes food plants from every continent in the world except for Antarctica.

Little Italy

DOWNTOWN TORONTO

The Essence

Farther along College is where Toronto's Italian community (and a lot of other folks) go to wine, dine and play. Street signs in the shape of Italy's "boot" mark the area. After dark, between brightly lit trees, clubs, cafés and bistros pulse with the beat of a nightlife that would seem to have no end. The air fills with the aroma of oregano, garlic, and basil as some of the best food and nightlife in Toronto starts cooking.

By day, the clubs clean up and life in the neighbourhood emerges. Named in tribute to the thousands of people of Italian descent who made the area at College and Euclid their home at the start of the early 1950s, Little Italy today is a melange of "urban cool", old-world Italian, and emerging artists.

While you're there, why not take an afternoon stroll in the Ossington Old Orchard Wilderness Garden, see a masterpiece on the dome of St. Anne's Church then have your tastebuds tantalized at one of the many hip restaurants on College between Bathurst and Christie?

The Roots —A Taste of History

As a commercial and residential focal point for Toronto's Italian community, the area around College and Ossington was just emerging as early as the 1920s. Larger numbers of Italian immigrants arrived after WWII. It wasn't long before Italian entrepreneurs set up shop and Little Italy was born.

By the 1960s, many of Little Italy's residents began to move north to the Corso Italia district on St. Clair West. Portuguese and South American families are still moving in to fill their place and add to the cultural mix Little Italy enjoys today. Italian restaurants and cafés still remain, as do the "social clubs", coffee shops and billiard halls filled with conversation, cigarette smoke and mostly older men discussing issues of the day, including the latest soccer scores.

Highlights

In addition to taking in Italian culture, visit these three highlights while your in the area.

OSSINGTON OLD ORCHARD WILDERNESS GARDEN (380 Ossington, 393-0710). Formerly a barren place of asphalt and stone, it is now a fertile oasis and an invaluable green asset to the area. In 1989, students, parents and teachers transformed their school grounds to include terraced gardens, an upland forest, a hedgerow aviary, a playing field and prairie meadow, and an apple orchard.

Evolving as a learning centre for children, the garden takes a critical step towards fostering an appreciation for the natural environment and has helped unite all the participants in something that is spiritually as well as socially rewarding. Everyone learns. They learn about gardening, working together and balancing their demands on nature and showing respect for the earth. It's a place where kindergarten children enjoy hot soup made from their own garden vegetable harvest.

Participate in community naturalization programs and tree planting from May to October! It's free and available to anyone. Call *Evergreen* at 596-1495 to find out the details, then show up with your grubby clothes and your enthusiasm.

ST. ANNE'S ANGLICAN CHURCH (270 Gladstone, near Dufferin at Dundas W., 536-3160). The interior dome of this 1908 church provided the palette for a lofty team including, among others, three members of the Group of Seven (Frank Carmichael, Fred Horsman Varley and lead painter J. E. H. Macdonald). Their vibrantly-coloured work chronicling the life of Christ is noted for its non-traditional Byzantine design. It was modelled by architect Fred Howland as a replica of the church of St. Sofia in Constantinople (now Istanbul).

DUFFERIN GROVE PARK (Dufferin, north of College). A gently sloping ravine defines the area where a mature grove of deciduous trees is criss-crossed by ample walkways in the centre and southern section of the park. In recent years, the blended talents of this culturally diverse neighbourhood have transformed the physical and social landscape. Today, a native and perennial plant garden, heritage vegetable and herb gardens, a marsh garden and a locally designed playground are flourishing. All gardens are planted and tended by locals. Two custom-crafted outdoor communal brick bake ovens have become the focal point for the neighbourhood, with their offerings of homemade bread and pizza on-site (see Photo section).

Audiences are drawn from across the city to see workshops and performances by "Clay and Paper Theatre", "The Stiltwalkers of Swizzlestick" theatre.

Dufferin Grove, as well as Trinity-Bellwoods and Winthrow neighbourhood parks are the settings for the spellbinding summertime twilight presentations of Dusk Dances by innovative Toronto dance artists. The natural environment serves as both stage and inspiration. The Friends of Dufferin Grove Park group encourages original community proposals for even more park activities and projects.

Things to Do, See, Buy & Eat

This whole area is a gold mine of Italian food and bars — let your nose lead you to the restaurant of your choice.
FRUITION CAFÉ & JUICE BAR (492 College, 920-5428). Delicious, healthy fruit and veggie drinks, good sandwiches, salads and crepes.
JOHN'S CLASSIC ITALIAN PIZZA (591 College, 537-0598). Great classic Italian pizza!
ROYAL - REPERTORY CINEMA (606 College, 516-4845). Once slated for demolition to make room for a parking lot, the Royal has been restored to its original art deco elegance, a classic silver screen theatre (comfy seats included) that serves as a venue for an annual film festival.
FOUND OBJECTS INTERNET CAFÉ (657 College, 588-9600). Also sells environmental art.
EL CONVENTO RICO (750 College, 588-7800). Music, dance and drag all combine at this eclectic inclusive club.

Carlton Street — Heading East

On the east side of Yonge, College becomes Carlton. This short road runs six city blocks to Parliament and across the north end of Cabbagetown. (See page 75.) During its rather short journey, it engages briefly with one of Toronto's defining characteristics, the vibrant lesbian and gay presence on Church Street.

Church–Wellesley Village

The Essence

Want to go hang out where it's comfortable to be gay, lesbian, bisexual, transgendered or transsexual? Head north along Church from Carlton. Exploring the four blocks up to Wellesley takes you through Toronto's most openly lesbian and gay settings.

Toronto has one of the largest lesbian and gay populations in North America. The intersection of Church and Wellesley is its hub. It's a magnet for people seeking to escape bigotry and discrimination. Year-round, events focus on social issues, fund-raising, and above all, community spirit and pride. Community press, phone lines, bulletin boards and lamp posts all carry the news of current happenings.

Church itself is about shopping, pubbing and dining. Although many of the businesses and services are gay and lesbian-oriented, this is a neighbourhood shared by everyone. For blocks around in any direction, the side streets are quiet and tree-lined, making it a great place for walking around.

The principal difference here is that no one assumes everyone is heterosexual. And non-heterosexuals aren't just accepted here, they are celebrated. If you like the idea of a strong, comfortable neighbourhood with room for all — come to Church and Wellesley.

The Roots — A Taste of History

For some time, there has been a lesbian and gay presence in this part of town. But since the early 70s, it's become more and more visible.

Early lesbian and gay pride celebrations became a summer staple of the neighbourhood and now, half a million people or more spend a week in June in an outpouring of mutual respect, goodwill, and good cheer. Community services and community press with a lesbian and gay focus also evolved here. In addition to more traditional offerings, the community centre at 519 Church (see below) began years ago to host lesbian and gay programs not found anywhere else in town.

To top this off, architectural delights abound. This is an old Toronto neighbourhood with a who's-who of historically significant residents and their fine houses.

Highlights

519 CHURCH STREET COMMUNITY CENTRE
(519 Church, 392-6874). Known now as a gathering place for gay and lesbian support, activity and action groups, the 519 is a great place to check out if you want information about what's going on in the neighbourhood. It was originally built in 1906 as part of the Granite Curling Club. The low wall on the north side of the park was the original outer wall of the curling rink.

CAWTHRA PARK AND AIDS MEMORIAL (Church and Wellesley, behind 519 Church). Known locally as the Church beach because so many community members sunbathe here. Community theatre and a broad range of events and activities take over the park on summer evenings. A curving path departs the main walk way through the park and leads past slender granite columns with plaques bearing the names of people who have died from AIDS.

Things to Do, See, Buy & Eat

PRIDE WEEK/PARADE TORONTO (927-7433). A full week of celebration at the end of June.

ARMEN ART GALLERY (16 Wellesley W., 924-5375). Features a diverse collection of North American Native art with a focus on Canadian artworks.

GLAD DAY BOOK SHOP (598A Yonge, 961-4161). Canada's oldest gay and lesbian bookshop.

THE BODY SHOP (71 Wellesley E., 323-1878). Cosmetics and body care that also cares for the environment. Many locations throughout Toronto.

CAWTHRA SQUARE CAFÉ (519 Church, 392-6878). Mostly vegetarian menu.

PLANET EARTH (473 Church, 929-2007). Preservative-free and home made cosmetics.

NATIONAL BALLET SCHOOL (105 Maitland, 964-3780). A 1911 Quaker meeting hall reminiscent of a civil war era southern mansion or the entrance to a European concert hall. It now houses Canada's national dance company school.

O'CONNOR GALLERY (97 Maitland, 921-7149). Showcasing gay and lesbian art.

KUALI (7 Maitland, 923-0925). Malaysian eatery with vegetarian delights.

BUDDIES IN BAD TIMES THEATRE (12 Alexander, 975-8555). Featuring Canadian content, often dealing with lesbian and gay issues and themes.

MAPLE LEAF GARDENS (60 Carlton, 977-1641). Walk past the last surviving building from hockey's 'original six'. "The Gardens" was a historical shrine for Toronto hockey fans for more than 65 years. As long as it stands the roof will span the ice surface. Not just recently, the roof spans the entire space so no one is forced to sit behind a post. Hockey games are now held at the Air Canada centre.

Bloor Street / Danforth Avenue

Bloor runs west from the Don Valley. Danforth runs east from the Don Valley. The Prince Edward Viaduct linked them way back in 1918. (See page 101.)

Central Bloor is the top of downtown. To the west Bloor hits hot spots all the way along. Along Danforth major shopping and major communities highlight the way.

A subway line runs from Bloor and Kipling in the far western reaches to Danforth and Victoria Park in the east before taking off northeast. The subway makes this an easy street to travel. Choose your spots and hit the rails.

To get a view of Toronto's great green expanses, go up to the restaurant Panorama (967-0000) on the 51st floor of the Manulife Centre at Bay and Bloor. You can look north to leafy Rosedale and the Don Valley or south to the Toronto Islands and beyond.

Bloor Street — Heading West

Yorkville

A block north of Bloor, east from Yonge to Avenue. This is the place to start if you're already downtown.

The Essence

Grandiose decadence, historical integrity and a tribute to the Canadian ecosystem. Where else can you find it all in a few short blocks?

Here, opulent lodgings, luxurious office towers, four star hotels, gourmet restaurants, a prestigious shopping district, VIP movie theatre, and side-streets replete with picture perfect Victorian homes are all grouped within two or three blocks. Yorkville and Cumberland are the ultimate in consumerism and material excess. The many laneways between these streets are reminiscent of the narrow passageways of older European cities and are peppered with restaurants and boutiques.

North, not two minutes away, is a storybook community with perfectly preserved architectural gems from Yorkville's inception. And just where Yorkville ends to the south, there, covering a subway tunnel, is a work of environmental art that might take you by surprise.

The Roots — A Taste of History

A community existed here at the town of York boundaries in the very early 1800s. The earliest business in the area was the tollgate where Yonge entered town at Bloor. Then, breweries and brick works opened nearby, attracting more settlers. Eventually the Village of Yorkville was incorporated in 1853 (Look for the village coat of arms that can be seen on the firehall on Yorkville Street).

Yorkville was a country retreat where the well-to-do escaped city drudgery while still staying relatively close at hand (and paying much lower taxes).

Transforming from a bedroom community and growing commercial centre, by the 1960s Yorkville had given itself over to the counter culture of the flower-child. Just down the way from a pedestrianized, hippy-ized Yonge Street intimate folk clubs opened in the tiny living rooms of 19th century houses of Yorkville. Then as the tempestuous days of the Vietnam War drew to a close, hippy culture vanished from the scene and Yorkville regained its composure and slowly began the upscale climb.

Artists and artisans began to exhibit in cafés-cum-galleries. Coffee houses changed signage, acquired chefs and evolved into bistros. Renovation restored some of the gutted clubs that made great new homes for expensive antiques and designer clothing. The era of Yorkville chic had arrived, and seems set for the long haul.

Highlights

RAMSDEN PARK (Yonge at Pears, 392-1111). Just below the surface of this park (in addition to Castle Creek) is a wet soil used make a particular kind of white brick that you can see in the St. James Cathedral. (See page 57.)

Ramsden Park was the site of one of the largest brickyards in the city. Looking west from Yonge down Belmont, you can see a row of houses that mark the border wall of the brickyard. To the north, it extended to Walker (near St. Clair). If it's raining, your feet may get soaked — the moisture on a dry day is only 6cm (2 inches) below the surface.

VILLAGE OF YORKVILLE PARK (Bellair and Cumberland, 392-1111). On the south side of Cumberland running west from the corner of Bellair, a remarkable park / sculpture / space has been created by landscape artist Martha Schwartz.

Represented here on less than 0.4 hectares (one acre) of land is the entire Canadian landscape: pine grove, prairie, marsh, orchard and a granite rock outcropping weighing 650 tonnes. Look closely and see the cracks that have been cemented together. The rock from Northern Ontario was broken into pieces for transportation and then put together again. The park was designed as a series of gardens varying in width, with frames symbolic of the lot lines of the row of houses that once stood on the site.

FIRE HALL NUMBER 10 (34 Yorkville). Built before annexation, and bearing the Yorkville coat of arms on its tower, this is still a working station. The coat of arms displays the initial and symbol of the profession of the first councillors: a beer barrel for the brewer, a jack plane for the carpenter, a brick mould for the brickmaker, an anvil for the blacksmith and a bull's head for the butcher.

BLOOR STREET WEST

Things to Do, See, Buy & Eat

CHURCH OF THE REDEEMER (162 Bloor W., 922-4948). Nestled next to a monolithic glass and steel office building, the severe, no-nonsense exterior hides exquisite High Victorian ornamentation inside.

HAZELTON LANES (55 Avenue Rd., 968-8600). Upscale shopping galore. Enclosed mall with a courtyard.

HELICONIAN CLUB (35 Hazleton, 922- 3618). This historical wooden-structured private women's club is preserved exactly as it existed when built in 1876.

ISSACS/INUIT GALLERY (9 Prince Arthur, 921-9985). Canadian and Inuit art.

MIRA GODARD GALLERY (22 Hazelton, 964-8197). One of Toronto's oldest commercial galleries featuring Canadian and international art.

YORKVILLE PUBLIC LIBRARY (22 Yorkville, 393-7660). This 1907 Carnegie Library was remodelled in 1976. It retains its original feel while being a fully-equiped modern library.

OMEGA CENTRE BOOKSTORE (29 Yorkville, 975-9086). Great alternative bookstore.

MORI (1280 Bay, 961-1094). Great, inexpensive Japanese noodle bar and sushi house with vegetarian offerings.

GREG'S ICE CREAM (200 Bloor W., 961-4734). Greg's home made ice cream is yummy!

WANDA'S PIE IN THE SKY (7A Yorkville, 925-7437). Vegetarian sandwiches and unbelievable pies.

Visitor Information

BLOOR YORKVILLE BUSINESS IMPROVEMENT ASSOCIATION (55 Bloor W., Suite 220, 928-3553). Info kiosks outside the Royal Ontario Museum and at Bloor and Yonge during the summer.

Approximately 250,000 aquatic and herbacious trees and shrubs have been planted in the city over the past nine years. [13]

The Annex

North of Bloor, the Annex runs from Bathurst to Avenue Rd. and then up to Dupont. It covers everything south of Bloor from Spadina to Grace and south to College.

The Essence

Here are streets that beg to be strolled. Not only an architectural wonderland, it holds an abundance of magnificent greenery and beautiful gardens. Many homes date from the mid to late 1800s.

Fully restored mansions and quaint turn-of-the-century cottages stand side by side, block after block. Grandeur and a sense of excess are evident in some of the properties. Imagine them as they would have appeared when they were new. Now hundred-year-old trees line the streets and give the Annex a timeless feel.

Brunswick Ave. is writer's haven — many a book or story has been written in and about these Annex homes.

These neighbourhoods are among Toronto's most diverse and inclusive. Annex residents are of many ethnic, racial and cultural backgrounds representing business, the arts, academe, and people who crave a return to a neighbourly style of inner-city life.

The Annex's long-time neighbour, the University of Toronto (see page 78), lends the neighbourhood a vaguely torn-jeans radical-meets-pipe-and-leather-patches air as students and faculty hustle between home, school, café and pub. There is also vibrant life after dark. There's always a buzz from the bars, restaurants and nightclubs that crowd together along Bloor Street.

The Roots — A Taste of History

Subdivided between the 1850s and 1880s, the Annex immediately became an elite Toronto neighbourhood.

North of Bloor early area residents included the likes of department store patriarch Timothy Eaton and George Gooderham, president of the Gooderham and Worts Distillery. To the south, developers highlighted proximity to the new Parliament Buildings and the benefits of a superior elevation as selling points for families seeking a restrained and serene urban lifestyle.

By the late 1920s, the wealthiest families began to migrate northward to newer, more fashionable suburbs in Forest Hill (see page 92) and Lawrence Park. Most of the large mansions were then renovated as rooming houses and multi-unit homes. The Annex and South Annex took on a whole new character during WWII and the years following. A bohemian atmosphere prevailed into the 1970s as students, artists, musicians, writers, and people of moderate means dominated. These days, many of the original Annex mansions are being restored as single family houses.

There are 3 million trees in Toronto on public streets and in parks alone. Trees shade us, absorb CO_2, produce oxygen, save energy, lessen the need for air conditioning and provide homes for millions of birds and other species. [14]

Highlights

BATA SHOE MUSEUM (327 Bloor W., 979-7799). See 4,500 years of shoe history and you'll understand that to practice the most sustainable form of transportation in style, the right shoes are a must! This museum proudly displays Robert Redford's cowboy boots, Terry Fox's running shoe and Queen Victoria's ballroom slippers.

SPADINA HOUSE AND GARDENS (285 Spadina Rd., 392-6910). These beautiful Victorian and Edwardian gardens cover 2.5 hectares (6 acres) and include more than 300 varieties of flowers and vegetables. Operated as a museum year-round, **Spadina House** offers a glimpse of the life and times of financier James Austin and his family, who occupied it for four generations (see Photo section).

In the summer, Sunday musical performances resound in the orchard. This is a great site for special events, and it provides a popular set for the film industry.

To get here, head up the Baldwin steps two blocks north from Dupont subway, or take the 127 bus N from Spadina Station to Davenport. Adults $5, seniors / youths $4, children $3.50.

CASA LOMA (1 Austin Terrace, near Davenport and Kendall, 923-1171). Casa Loma is a medieval-looking castle perched just north of the northern extreme of the Annex. This former home of Canadian financier and military officer Sir Henry Pellatt was built between 1911 and 1914. It has secret passageways, a treasure-trove of Pellatt heirlooms, real castle charm and 2 hectares (5 acres) of stunning gardens with roses, rare native wildflowers, colourful rhododendrons, azaleas and old-fashioned perennial borders (all thanks to the members of the Garden Club of Toronto who raised $1.5 million for the garden renovations). Nearby, an 240 metre (800-foot) tunnel connects the 98 room castle to the stables.

Casa Loma

CITY OF TORONTO ARCHIVES (255 Spadina Rd., 392-5000). Opened in 1992, the records stored here include over one million photographs, thousands of maps and hundreds of other special collections all documenting various aspects of Toronto's history. The Archives makes available a range of public programs and ever-changing exhibits and theatre presentations that provide a context for understanding the City of Toronto, its current issues and future directions.

See the computerized storage facility or view archival records in the Research Hall.

FOREST HILL (Spadina and St. Clair W). While you're in the area, venture a little further north to Forest Hill village. Forest Hill was incorporated as a village in 1923. It was named after the summer residence of John Wickson, built in 1860, at the junction of Eglinton W. and Old Forest Hill Road. The hill is still there, but the forest is long since gone, having been replaced by apartment buildings.

Prior to its incorporation, Forest Hill had been known as "Spadina Heights". Spadina is a derivative of the First Nations word "Ishapadenah", which means a hill or sudden rise of land. The boundaries of the present day neighbourhood are shaped from the old Spadina Heights school district.

"Lower Forest Hill", south of Eglinton, was completely developed by the 1930s. "Upper Forest Hill" was slower to develop due to the fact it had previously been occupied by the old Belt Line railway, and then by industry.

In 1967, Forest Hill Village joined Swansea Village as

one of the last two independent villages to be annexed by the City of Toronto.

The Forest Hill neighbourhood is one of Toronto's most prestigious districts. The mansions in Lower Forest Hill are rivalled only by those found in Rosedale. Forest Hill's schools are among the best in the country. They include two of Canada's most revered private schools: Upper Canada College for boys, and Bishop Strachan School for girls.

Forest Hill is one of Toronto's prettier districts. Its topography is very diverse with gently sloping hills, winding roads, and numerous little parkettes all adding charm to the neighbourhood.

KARMA FOOD CO-OP (739 Palmerston, 534-1470). A thriving non-profit co-operative food store founded in 1972. Their mission includes fostering a healthy connection to the food we eat and the people who grow it, cultivating active community and co-operative education on environmental issues and exercising political and economic control over our food. It carries a wide range of organic health food and natural products including: dairy, bulk grains, seeds, spreads, organic meat and more. You can join as a member or on a day-by-day basis for guest shopping to try it out.

Things to Do, See, Buy & Eat

NOAH'S NATURAL FOODS AND SUNNY CAFÉ (322 Bloor W., 968-7930). Health food supermarket with organic food and cafe.

NATIVE CANADIAN CENTRE (16 Spadina Rd., 964-9087). Native Centre and craft shop offers Drum Social Thursdays from 6-9 pm.

GRASSROOTS ENVIRONMENTAL PRODUCTS (408 Bloor W., 944-1993). One stop environmental shop providing healthy, earth-friendly products.

POOR ALEX THEATRE (296 Brunswick, 324-9863). Performances include theatre and dance and shows change weekly.

TRINITY ST. PAUL CHURCH (427 Bloor W., 922-4954). Place of worship, music concerts and community activities. Home to 15 community group offices.

KENSINGTON NATURAL BAKERY (460 Bloor W., 534-1294). Here, you can get a big tofu dinner special for less than $5.

ETERNAL MOMENTS (497 Bloor W., 924-3780). Bookstore and boutique focusing on personal development with a touch of the mystic!

BLOOR CINEMA (506 Bloor W., east of Bathurst, 516-2330). (See page 41 for other repertory cinema info.)
JUICE FOR LIFE (521 Bloor W., 531-2635). Gourmet juice bar and vegan restaurant — they also give compost away to local residents who request it for their gardens.
LEE'S PALACE (529 Bloor W., 532-1598). Check out the art mural outside and the live music venue inside.
GRAPEFRUIT MOON (968 Bathurst, 534-9056). Serves organic beef hamburgers and other yummy munchables.
ANNAPURNA (1085 Bathurst, 537-8513). Vegetarian Sri Lankan delights in a calming and restful atmosphere.
HONEST ED'S (581 Bloor W., 537-1574). Bargain store. (Have you ever seen so many lights?) It's a corner landmark. You have to go there to believe it — and you may pick up a bargain! Of course Honest Ed could save energy by changing from a 100-watt to a 20-watt circular lightbulb — and save about 8 cents a day too (we're sure he would like that part!).
TARRAGON (30 Bridgman, near Dupont and Bathurst, 531-1827). Its mainstage features a range of known Canadian playwrights as well as classics including Tennessee Williams.
INDIAN RICE FACTORY (414 Dupont, 961-3472). Received awards from NOW Magazine and Toronto Life for "favorite Indian food". High veggie content.
WONDERWORKS (79A Harbord, 323-3131). Books on the Goddess, sacred traditions, relaxation, meditation, creativity, alternative health and green economy.

High Park Neighbourhood

The Essence

The heart of this area is High Park, and the feel of its natural, controlled wilderness extends into the surrounding neighbourhoods. One block east of Parkside Dr., Indian Rd. (once part of a network of native trails that linked Lake Ontario with Lake Simcoe) features large homes on spacious lots fronting onto wide, winding streets with beautiful trees. Gently rolling hills support towering oak trees. Life here is a synthesis of the best of urban and country elements. The grandeur of Edwardian and Victorian architecture shares space with many smaller homes.

North of the Park along Bloor small shops offer a wide range of merchandise, gourmet foods, and salon services. There are all sorts of restaurants, corner fruit markets and delis. Year-round, High Park is frequented by locals and visitors from afar seeking succour from the stress of urban life.

One of Toronto's oldest and largest parks, High Park was deeded to the City of Toronto by architect John Howard in 1873 in perpetuity, as public parkland. [15]

The Roots — A Taste of History

John George Howard emigrated to York in 1832, becoming the city's first surveyor. He purchased lakefront property in 1836, naming his estate High Park because of its magnificent view of Lake Ontario. He called his home Colborne Lodge, after Lieutenant-Governor Sir John Colborne, who had appointed him drawing master at Upper Canada College.

After an unsuccessful attempt to develop the land, he deeded it to the city in exchange for an annual pension. On his death in 1873, High Park became the property of the City of Toronto. Howard's holdings comprise approximately one third of today's park. The balance is made up of two land acquisitions. One from the Rideout family (to the east) and in 1930, another from the Chapmans' (to the west).

Highlights

HIGH PARK (Keele and Bloor, 392-1111). High Park is the only area in Southern Ontario to combine the woodlands, wetlands and rare oak savannah habitats, once common throughout Toronto. On almost 160 hectares (400 acres) of public parkland, it stretches from Bloor south to the lakeshore. The park includes a fishing pond, animal paddocks, picnic areas, playgrounds, a restaurant, a historic museum, horticultural displays, a children's garden, and a scenic, trackless train (seasonal).

It also has skating and canoeing on Grenadier pond, as well as tennis in the park, and an extensive trail network. You can almost forget entirely that you are in a big city! A children's summer gardening program and guided and self-guided tours and hikes are just a few of the options for short or longer term visitors.

Four of the 41 rare plant species in High Park — wood betony, St. John's Wort, wild lupine, and cup-plant — are found in only four other places in Canada. [16]

High Park's vegetation is transitional between the Carolinean zone, a floristic region that reaches its northeasterly limit near Toronto, and the mixed hardwood zone, which extends north and east through central Ontario and Quebec. The Carolinean zone contains a high percentage of endangered habitats in Canada and approximately 65% of Ontario's rare species. The black oak savannah that dominates the park's sandy uplands is the most significant natural area remaining on the City's Iroqouis Sand Plain. Its open woodlands are remnants of the tallgrass prairie and savannah ecosystems that once dotted southern Ontario. High Park is the largest remnant in the region.

High Park's oak savannahs are now in danger because of the majority of its oak trees have reached maturity, are diseased, and are not regenerating. There is much restoration work going on, including invasive plant removal, planting and prescribed burn management. For more information call 338-0338 to request a copy of the document titled "Restoration Strategies for High Park".

There are approximately 8,000 hectares (20,000 acres) of green space in Toronto. [17]

Hawk hill is a great place to watch raptor bird migration anytime from September to November. Or just gaze at the stars at night.

Throughout the summer High Park is home to a variety of festivals, concerts, cycling races, and theatre.

If you want to learn more about the park, sign up for a High Park Walking Tour (392-1748). Nature-lovers can join the High Park Volunteer Stewardship Program, which aims to beautify the park in a guided program of weeding, planting and seed harvesting of indigenous plants. There are also open-air train tours throughout the summer for a nominal fee.

Why not pack a picnic, fly a kite, have a game of tennis or walk the woodland trails? You'll never explore it all in one day!

WITHIN HIGH PARK:

ADVENTURE PLAYGROUND (Parkside Dr. entrance, south of Bloor). A children's playground that resulted from the volunteer energy of more than 3,000 people including 1,000 imaginative drawings by children and a variety of contributions by local artists & craftspeople.

HILLSIDE GARDENS (West side of park.) The beautiful

natural scenery here includes the Hanging Gardens which are sunken gardens flanked by ephemeral cherry blossom trees.

GRENADIER POND (South end of park.) A blending of benign engineering intervention and selective shoreline plantings is restoring the complex ecology of this precious and beautiful body of water.

THE ANIMAL PADDOCK (South central section of the park.) Deer have been kept here since 1890. Now you can also visit bison, llamas, highland cattle and sheep year-round. Open 7am–8pm daily.

COLBORNE LODGE (1 Colborne Lodge Dr. in High Park, 392-6916). An elegant regency-style cottage built in 1837 for the Howards, the park's founders and original owners. It boasts one of Toronto's first indoor bathrooms. The popular Harvest Festival held here in October features music, storytelling, seasonal fare and nature hikes. Guided tours are available.

High Park has Toronto's only solar powered telephone (for emergency calls only). [18]

DISCOVERY WALK — WESTERN RAVINES & BEACHES (High Park, Keele and Bloor, 392-1111). High Park subway Station at Bloor is the ideal place to start this walk. You will move south toward the east side of Grenadier Pond where boating and catch-and-release fishing (to maintain fish populations) are enjoyed all summer. Follow along to the Western Beaches and boardwalk where you can make your way west to the Humber Pedestrian Bridge (see Photo section) and Humber Bay Park or east to the Sunnyside Pool. Then head north along the west side of Grenadier Pond through ravines and past fish ponds back up to Bloor Street.

BLOOR WEST VILLAGE. Just north and west of High Park is one of the city's distinct neighbourhoods. Its past includes a strong East European influence that is still felt today in the many Ukrainian and Polish businesses located there. Quaint cafés, distinctive bakeries, delis and restaurants abound, making this a great place to meet friends for a leisurely cup of coffee.

If you feel an eco-urge coming on, why not look up the local enviro folks at the Bloor W. Eco-Village. (See page 151.)

SWANSEA. This neighbourly community and one-time village of Swansea south of Bloor took shape with the opening of the Bolt Works near Lakeshore in the 1880s, followed by the Stelco operation that closed in 1990. Visit the Swansea Town Hall (95 Lavinia) for info on local happenings.

Things to Do, See, Buy & Eat

GRENADIER CAFÉ AND TEAHOUSE (200 Parkside Dr., High Park, 769-9870). In addition to serving food, they recycle and have a natural environment committee.
THE DREAM IN HIGH PARK (367-8243). This program of Shakespearean works happens in July and August right inside High Park and was the first open-air Shakespearean theatre in Toronto.
HIGH PARK ALLOTMENT GARDENS (392-7291). Check out the beautiful plots planted and cared for by neighbourhood gardeners and resplendent with the colour and variety of vegetables and ornamentals.
BIRDERS NATURE STORE (2100 Bloor W., 604-9272). A field day for the backyard naturalist.
RUNNYMEDE LIBRARY (2178 Bloor W., 393-7697). A graceful and defining landmark at the east end of Bloor West Village.
VILLAGE PLAYHOUSE (2190 Bloor W., 767-9427). This 25 year old theatre presents a range of contemporary and classical repertoire, and is almost entirely volunteer-run.
KINGSWAY THEATRE - REPERTORY CINEMA (3030 Bloor W., 236-1411).

Bloor Street / Danforth Avenue — Heading East

Bloor runs east of Yonge to the Don Valley. Where it crosses the Prince Edward viaduct over the valley its name changes to the Danforth. Both streets connect to provide exploration opportunities as diverse as Rosedale, Moore Park ravine and Greektown.

Cyclists, runners, or in-line skaters can also connect with the network of trails just north of Danforth. Take Broadview north a few blocks and turn west onto Pottery Road. The trail begins just east of the bridge crossing the Don River. For more information about the Don River area, see page 128.

Rosedale

North of Bloor and east of Yonge is Rosedale, a luxurious neighbourhood superb for rambling among its beautiful architecture and sumptuous grounds.

The Essence

A Rosedale address is an address of distinction in Toronto and has been for over 100 years. Surrounded by palatial homes, beautiful ravines, gorgeous garden sanctuaries and parkland, you feel as though you are far from the city when in fact you're just a few minutes walk away.

Known for its winding, weaving streets, the easiest thing to do in Rosedale, and one of the nicest too, is to get lost. Meandering along the streets viewing gardens and architecture, from time to time you will come across a park where you can sit on a bench, rest your feet and try to figure out how to get back to where you started.

The Roots — A Taste of History

Rosedale was the 1820 estate of Mary and Botsford Jarvis. After 1909, when a bridge was built to span Park Drive Ravine, the subdivision of these expensive lots into large tracts of land on wide meandering streets seemed the most logical way to extend the serenity and lush beauty for the benefit of the new owners.

These homes were within reach of only the most well-heeled of Toronto and remain so to this day.
Take the 82 Rosedale bus from Rosedale subway for a meandering round-trip look at the neighbourhood.

Highlights

MOORE PARK RAVINE (Moore Ave., east of Hudson Dr., 392-8186). The Central Ravines, Belt Line and Gardens Discovery Walk includes the Moore Park Ravine. This ravine is well known for its walking path and natural habitat areas. Its thickly wooded slopes and wetlands provide good opportunities for viewing birds and other wildlife.

The Ravine follows Mud Creek, a small tributary of the Don River. At one time water drawn from Mud Creek was used in the brick making process. The Don Valley Brick Works is located where much of the mud ended up, just east of the ravine (see page 132).

Moore Park Ravine can be entered from Moore east of Hudson Dr., or at the south end just west of Bayview or by a choice of pedestrian/ bicycle trails. (See the Green Tourism Association's *Other* Map of Toronto).

Things to Do, See, Buy & Eat

MAURICE CODY HALL (277 Bloor E., 961-8116). Built in 1861 as part of St. Paul's Anglican Church, it ranks among the best architecture in Toronto and is a venue for public readings of Shakespeare and other such happenings.

JARVIS STREET. Stroll south to Wellesley and view the former mansions of the Massey family and other contemporaries. The mansions have been converted into apartments, shops, theatres, restaurants and for various other uses.

REBEL HOUSE (1068 Yonge, 927-0704). Canadian food, a variety of beer on tap and a great atmosphere can be found in this wood planked old house.

ALL THE BEST FINE FOODS (1099 Yonge, 928-3330). Beautifully crafted prepared foods, baked goods and cheeses. Also has giftwares.

The Danforth

The Essence

Tourism and community coexist on "The Danforth", as it is locally known. They come closest between the Don Valley and Pape. In this stretch, there is a rich community that combines the zest of modern Mediterranean life with the distinctly historic spirit of ancient Greece. Further east, the atmosphere grows more Anglo, but still retains a small business, corner-store feel. Most of the homes in the area are set back from the street and many a homeowner takes great pride in their beautiful frontage. The annual self-guided "Secret Garden" tours in Riverdale offer a peak into backyard gardens too, but only in July.

Flanked by many neighbourhoods, the Danforth has been evolving since the turn of the century. To explore its whole length is to acquire a sense of how Toronto grew like concentric rings in the cross section of a tree, neighbourhood by neighbourhood.

The Roots — A Taste of History

Danforth begins at the Don Valley and continues east for about 10 kilometres until it merges with Kingston Rd. and disappears into the distance. The street was named for Asa Danforth, who built Kingston Rd. in 1799.

Communities began to dot the ditch-lined, dirt street through the 1800s. As more and more of Toronto's citizenry moved in, these many small communities flowed together. Between 1880 and 1924, homes of all sizes, mostly Victorian in style, were built. In the early 1900s the city began to annex these communities. By 1919 the Prince Edward Viaduct (see page 101) linked the Danforth to Toronto, and factories, market gardens and brickyards were displaced by residential housing. By the late 1960s, following the opening of the east-west Bloor-Danforth subway line, the Danforth was established as a system of neighbourhoods with a distinct change of personality every few subway stops.

Toronto Transit Commission (TTC) route maps are on display at all subway stations, and smaller copies are reprinted in the Toronto Yellow Pages telephone book. You can call 393-4636 for fares, routing information and schedules from 7 am to 10 pm 7 days a week. For more detailed TTC information, see page 27.

Highlights

GREEKTOWN ON THE DANFORTH. Feel like a taste of Athens? Since the 1950s, Greek immigrants have gravitated to this neighbourhood where they found compatriots with whom to share Greek language and culture while they acclimatised to their new home. Over time, they opened businesses that reflected the best of what they had left behind. Restaurants, taverns, bakeries, special cultural events, and all the ambience you could ask for are featured in Greektown. Outdoor patios line the streets in summer and make a great stop to catch your breath from exploring the shops. This colourful neighbourhood runs from Broadview to about Pape on both sides of Danforth Ave.

PRINCE EDWARD VIADUCT (where Bloor becomes Danforth). This magnificent bridge is known locally as the Bloor Viaduct. Construction, supervised by R. C. Harris, Commissioner of Public Works (namesake of the historic water filtration plant — see page 118), was completed in 1919. The first span is 60 metres long and crosses the Rosedale Ravine. The second span is 500 metres long and crosses the Don Valley.

Designed by Thomas Taylor, the viaduct included provision for future rapid transit on a lower level. This level is now used by the east-west subway line. Michael Ondaatje's book, *In the Skin of a Lion*, is beautifully poetic about the construction of this bridge, its role in Toronto mythology, and its dramatic inauguration featuring a cyclist.

CARROT COMMON (348 Danforth, 466-2129). This unique, more-than-a-neighbourhood shopping plaza has shops offering health food, alternative health care services, organically grown produce, and more zen-like retail. It is a unique partnership drawing on the talents of a worker co-op with expertise in organic foods, a co-op venture capital group, a private developer interested in community goals, a merchant banker, and local community advocacy groups.

More than 50% of the profits flow to community based organizations like Carrot Cache (a non-profit corporation set up to fund new worker-owned co-operatives and small organic farming projects); a venture capital fund operated by the Co-operative Resource Pool of Ontario, the Jesuit Centre and Citizens for Public Justice; as well as to a fund that supports social justice and community economic development initiatives. Not surprisingly you can also pick up a copy of the *Vegetarian Directory* here.

DOWNTOWN TORONTO

Things to Do, See, Buy & Eat

MUSIC HALL - REPERTORY CINEMA (147 Danforth, 778-8272).

THE BIG CARROT (348 Danforth, 466-2129). Specializing in minimally processed, organically grown, cruelty-free and environmentally safe food and products.

GRASSROOTS ENVIRONMENTAL PRODUCTS (372 Danforth, 466-2841). Offers recycled office supplies, non-toxic personal care products, ecological garden alternatives, air and water filters, alternative energy appliances (check out their wind-up flashlights) and environmental books and magazines.

WITHROW PARK (Logan south of Danforth). Offers Performances of Dusk Dances and Shakespeare in the Rough as well as shady respites and gardens.

Dusk Dances — Outstanding dance artists performing 10-minute choreographed pieces inspired by the natural surroundings (see Photo section). Catch them on July evenings at dusk in Withrow Park, Trinity-Bellwoods Park and Dufferin Grove Park. Call 588-2210 for dates and locations.

TORONTO'S WATERFRONT

The Essence

After exhausting all the green and groovy possibilities in the bustling and intense downtown core, a return to the waterfront is a return to the source — the source of Toronto's very early history, the source of all of Toronto's drinking water and the source of a feeling of open and regenerative space.

If you sailed into Toronto from the east, you first glimpse the white matte of the imposing Scarborough Bluffs. Then appears a low-lying waterfront punctuated by neighbourhoods and parks. As you near the city's core, there arises the unmistakable presence of industry, old and new. To the west, parkland and natural areas again prevail.

For most of its two hundred years, Toronto existed as a port city that gave itself over to shipping. In time, and with few exceptions, it walled off the downtown waterfront from its people. Moving into the twenty-first century, it has forged a newer, stronger life in white collar commerce. Less is demanded of the waterfront and, for the most part, industry has fled the scene. Now, as though a stream, long buried, has finally found its way back to the surface, people are trickling back in. They are making space for themselves, and slowly reconnecting the city to the lake.

Parks and gardens have appeared where storage sheds once stood. Warehouses have become theatres, museums, and clubs. East and west of the core, stretches of shoreline are gradually being reclaimed and revitalized. Places for people and for nature are set across the Toronto shoreline like pearls in a necklace. Still, recovery is not yet complete. Toronto is faced with some very important decisions to make about waterfront health and happiness.

As an eco-tourist, you can play a role in waterfront recovery. Call the Toronto Waterfront Naturalization Initiative at 661-6600, x 5349. Find out about activities during your visit and plug in. For trail information visit www.tctrail.ca or call 1-800-465-3636.

The Roots — A Taste of History

For centuries before Europeans settled Toronto, native Canadians lived pretty much in harmony with the land,

WATERFRONT

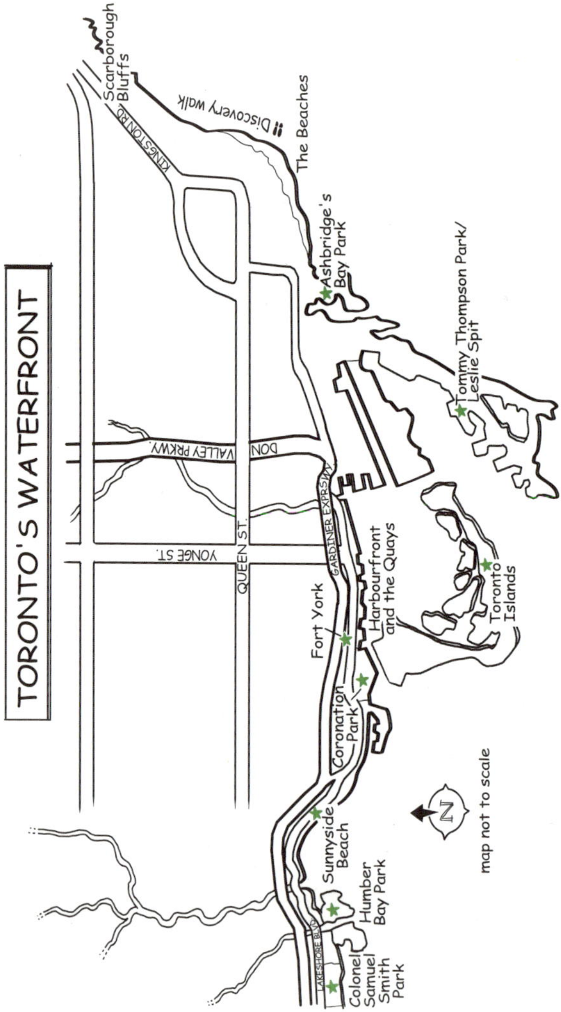
TORONTO'S WATERFRONT
Scarborough Bluffs
Discovery walk
The Beaches
KINGSTON RD.
Ashbridge's Bay Park
Tommy Thompson Park/ Leslie Spit
DON VALLEY PRKWY.
YONGE ST.
QUEEN ST.
GARDINER EXPRSWY
Harbourfront and the Quays
Toronto Islands
Fort York
Coronation Park
Sunnyside Beach
Humber Bay Park
LAKESHORE BLVD.
Colonel Samuel Smith Park
N
map not to scale

allowing it to guide them in its use. Continuing into the nineteenth century, the trails they followed served as overland trade and transportation routes and, today, survive in part as the basis for some city streets. The rivers, streams, and creeks became their highways and, along with Lake Ontario, a source for life-sustaining food and drinking water.

When explorers arrived, they too saw that this wholesome land could provide for their survival. But as their numbers grew, their approach to development took an unfortunate toll.

In the European explorer's experience of overcrowded cities, towns and villages, it had been necessary to make the land conform to their needs. Here, in their new land, forest was cleared and sectioned to suit industry and settlement, driving plant and animal life to the margins. Waterways were diverted, clogged with freshly-cut trees and used as garbage disposals by communities and all manner of industry. Many became so poisoned that their waters were unsafe to touch, let alone drink.

Today's waterfront exists over once-marshy wetland born of rivers and streams as they eased their way to silt-rich deltas. Humid and damp by summer, these waterfront swamps were seen as a disease-carrying threat and a barrier to development. Plans to dump landfill and dry out the waterfront met with no resistance. Civilization overwhelmed nature at almost every turn. Only recently has the need for responsible water management been recognized. Today, much time and a great deal of money are spent trying to put right what went so wrong.

WATERFRONT TRAILS

Martin Goodman Trail. This 22-kilometre Toronto segment of Ontario's Waterfront Trail leads cyclists, marathon trainers, joggers, and skaters along the Lake Ontario shoreline past strikingly beautiful parks and beaches against a skyline backdrop. Gently lapping waves beseech travellers to pause and enjoy the lake's beauty.

A side trip to the Toronto Islands (see page 109) is something you can fit in for a few hours, although you will wish you had set aside a whole day.

Going eastward, the trail dips south down Cherry, across a suspension bridge and through Cherry Beach, a little waterfront miracle. This serene, wooded tract of meadowlands grew out of landfill once designated for industrial purposes. It is now one of the cleanest beaches along the waterfront and a popular place for enjoying the natural shoreline, sailboarding, or enjoying a quiet, romantic pause.

At Leslie, you can take a side trip south to **Tommy Thompson Park**, (see page 115), or you can carry on to Ashbridge's Bay Park and the Beaches. (See page 116).

Ontario's Waterfront Trail. Extending from Toronto's Martin Goodman Trail, Ontario's Waterfront Trail follows the shore of Lake Ontario for 325 kilometres from Niagara-on-the-Lake east to Trenton. It connects with the Seaway Trail in the United States which runs along the south shores of Lakes Ontario and Erie.

TransCanada Trail. The TransCanada Trail, a permanent path winding clear across Canada, does a loop coming down Yonge crossing the Martin Goodman Trail and carrying on through Exhibition Place and all the way to Niagara Falls, Ontario.

WATERFRONT

Toronto has 7,000 hectares of parks. Three-quarters of them are ravines, valleylands, woodlots and waterfront natural areas. [19]

Harbourfront and the Quays

Harbourfront is a great place to start to get to know Toronto's waterfront. You can get to any part of this central and booming hub of arts, crafts and active living by taking a short but exciting streetcar ride from Union station towards Exhibition Place, past blue water vistas and striking heritage sites. Better still, grab a bike and take advantage of the opportunities for meandering.

The Essence

Harbourfront, originally a port and industrial area, interrupts the Martin Goodman Trail mid-way in its reach across the waterfront. This is a place for people-watching if there ever was one. Spread out between Yonge and Bathurst, this area is a mix of waterfront walkways, marinas, modern residential and commercial towers, public squares and open-air stages all competing for attention. Once rundown warehouses, Queen's and York Quays include antique markets, theatres and festivals, hubs of arts and culture, one-of-a- kind shops, restaurants, galleries and studios. The Power Plant Gallery, Du Maurier Theatre, and Harbourfront Centre's Premier Dance Theatre provide performance sites for local and internationally known Canadian dance troupes. Events happen here year-round, so it's always worth a visit.

Time, budget and weather permitting, river boats, tall ships and fishing boats all stand by, ready to take you out on a cruise.

Why not rent a bike or in-line skates to get to your destination today? Ask your accommodation concierge for public transportation options or bike rentals near you. (See page 27.)

The Roots — A Taste of History

When you're at Harbourfront, you're actually standing on garbage. Landfill is the foundation upon which all of Harbourfront rests. Throughout its growth years Toronto has worked hard to push the lake farther away. Along with garbage, wrecking debris and earth from excavation have all found their way to the lake's edge. The Toronto Port Authority building (60 Harbour) stands back about a two-minute walk from the lake, but waves once lapped at its main stairs and visitors could tie up their boats to the mooring posts.

Although originally intended for industrial use, Harbourfront has become largely a beachfront promenade with lots of shops and high-rise housing.

Highlights

HARBOURFRONT CENTRE (410 Queen's Quay W., 973-3000). The surrounding yacht slips, walkways, theatres, open-air stages, outdoor vendor market and shops make for a people-watchers paradise (see Harbourfront Map in Photo section). Inside, its artsy feel hides its past as an industrial building. Make sure to walk along west to discover the Nautical Adventure Centre. It explores the history of Toronto Harbour as well as boat building.

The annual Milk International Children's Festival of the Arts held here is the largest children's festival in Canada. The world-renowned International Festival of Authors, Creative Sweden, and Worlds of Asia are just a few of the theme events that take place annually. Premier Dance Theatre presents dance troupes from all over the world and also features contemporary performing artists of every stripe. Hosting concerts and events all year-round, this is a weekend destination unto itself, particularly in the summer. Event admissions range from free to a nominal fee to ticketed.

ARTISTS' GARDENS (**Harbourfront Centre**, 235 Queens Quay W., 973-3000).These gardens showcase 15 very different themed gardens designed by 15 very different artists. These perennial plots feature visually stimulating blossoms and unique interpretations of nature, society, and gardening. Grab a pamphlet inside the Harbourfront Centre to lead you on a self-guided tour.

THE PIER: TORONTO'S WATERFRONT MUSEUM (245 Queen's Quay W., 338-7437). Taking up a fully restored 1930s shipping warehouse, this museum invites you to experience hands-on the unfolding story of the Toronto Harbour from the last ice age to the present day. Audio effects simulate all the noise of a busy harbour as the sounds and smells of Lake Ontario seep through to make it all the more real. You can also visit a real, working, wooden boat builder's workshop, take in some rare and historic marine art, or join a walking tour.

There's lots for kids here. Among other things, they can learn about canal locks and then dress up like a ship's captain, a pirate or an Edwardian lady. Open Mar – Oct, 10–4. Adults $5, seniors/children $4.

TORONTO MUSIC GARDEN (475 Queen's Quay W., between Bathurst and Spadina, over the bridge by the marsh). This is a divine and stirring garden inspired by Bach's Suites for Unaccompanied Cello. Internationally renowned cellist Yo Yo Ma and landscape designer Julie Moir Messervy rendered, in nature, a visual interpretation of this enchanting music. Each movement within the suite corresponds to a different section in the garden. This engaging setting is often complemented by storytellers, musical ensembles and dance performances. Architectural blacksmith Tom Tollefson fashioned the Music Pavilion, and Anne Roberts devised the Maypole.

Things to Do, See, Buy & Eat

REDPATH SUGAR MUSEUM (95 Queens Quay E., 366-3561). The factory facility is a refinery and the self-guided museum is housed inside. Open M-F 10-3:30 (call first). On the north side of the raw sugar shed there are murals of marine life created by artist Wyland.

GREAT LAKES SCHOONER (249 Queens Quay W., #111, 260-6355). Charters, day tours and educational programs.

QUEEN'S QUAY YACHTING (275 Queen's Quay W., 203-3000). Learn to crew on a yacht. Rentals also available

HARBOURFRONT ADVENTURE TOURS & CANOE & KAYAK SCHOOL (283A Queens Quay W., 203-2277).

Sign up for a lesson, or just take a kayak out for a paddle to get another perspective.

HARBOURFRONT ANTIQUE MARKET (400 Queens Quay W., 260-2626). Canada's largest antique market.

POWER PLANT CONTEMPORARY ART GALLERY (**Harbourfront Centre**, 231 Queen's Quay W., 973-4949). Always stimulating exhibits to explore.

TORONTO MISSION SEAFARERS (469-5391). If it's Thursday, it won't break your budget to enjoy lunch at the Port Authority. Have a chat with Father David Mulholland who has been with the Seafarers for over 25 years.

TRILLIUM PADDLEBOAT (392-8188). The only operating steam-powered, side paddlewheel ship in North America offers a cruise around the harbour (Mid-May to mid-Oct).

Visitor Information

TOURISM TORONTO (See page 18.)

Toronto Islands

The Essence

A quick ferry ride glides you across the harbour to this car-free paradise. Definitely think about spending a day and bringing a picnic lunch, or you can always opt for an Island restaurant. Didn't bring a bike with you on the ferry? You can rent one right here (go to Centre Island's pier). There's no better way to scout all that the Islands have to offer.

Six different plant communities and some of the last remnants of natural Lake Ontario shoreline make this a place to lose yourself in exploration. There are attractive landscaped gardens and wild, natural spaces all overflowing with colour. The historic 19th century Gibraltar Point Lighthouse, and its grim, well-kept secret, is worth a visit too (see page 111).

Be sure to make your way east to Algonquin and Ward's Islands. People have lived here since the 1800s. In the early 1900s, a community grew as people built year-round homes and cottages. In the mid-1900s, islanders were threatened with eviction to make way for an amusement park.

Heated battles boiled over in the City of Toronto council chambers. When all the dust settled, development plans were abandoned and a strong, unified community remained. This is a tribute to what a determined community can achieve. Stroll through the rustic, narrow lanes and feel the pride here. Just to the west is Hanlan's Point, named for competitive rower Ned Hanlan, one of Canada's first internationally known athletes.

Hanlan's Point includes Toronto's only clothing-optional beach. [20]

Pedestrian and bicycle trails criss-cross the Islands and the boardwalk on Ward's island is a cyclist's delight. You can take in the breathtaking views of the lake from the pier beside the bike rental at the bottom of Centre Island's formal gardens. Bike and boat rentals are also available, and there are quite a few picnic spots, some with fire pits (permit required).

If you want to play, choose among the beaches, softball diamonds, volleyball and tennis courts, and the Frisbee golf course. For the kids, there's a wading pool and amusement park. Got your own boat? Tie up at one of the public moorings (48-hour limit).

Toronto offers some good paddling. Try the Islands, Leslie Spit or along the Humber River. Didn't bring your canoe or kayak? Rent one at Harbourfront.

The Roots — A Taste of History

The Toronto Islands were not always islands. They were a series of continuously moving sandbars originating from the Scarborough Bluffs and carried westward by Lake Ontario currents. Many of the different herbs still growing here are the legacy of a Great Lakes Indian culture that saw in the Islands a sacred place of healing. All tribes were welcomed here provided that they first lay down arms.

By the early 1800s, the longest of the sandbars extended nearly 9 kilometres south west from Woodbine Ave., through Ashbridge's Bay and the marshes of the lower Don River, forming a natural harbour between the lake and the mainland. Before the islands completely separated, a popular carriage path from York that led to Gibraltar Point at the western tip of the peninsula also followed the shoreline east to Scarborough Bluffs.

Finally, in 1858, an island was created when a storm completely separated the peninsula from the mainland and the gap was not repaired. The Eastern Gap has since become an important shipping entrance into Toronto Harbour.

Highlights

Call Toronto Parks (392-8186, x 4) for information on the Islands.

GIBRALTAR POINT LIGHTHOUSE (Hanlan's Point) Built in 1809, this is the oldest lighthouse on the Great Lakes (see Photo section). It is no longer operating but has gained notoriety as the site of an infamous murder. J. P. Rademuller, Gibraltar's first attendant, died under mysterious and somewhat gory circumstances. Lots of speculation, but insufficient evidence leaves the crime unsolved to this day. Visitors can look over the scene and develop their own theories.

If you're itching for more historical depth, read the diary of Elizabeth Simcoe, wife of upper Canada's first Lieutenant-Governor. It includes an extensive account of native peoples, early settlement, and lost villages. [21]

Things to Do, See, Buy & Eat

TORONTO ISLAND FERRY (9 Queens Quay W., 392-8193). The ferry ride from island to island is a great thing to do even if you don't have time to land.

AVENUE OF THE ISLANDS GARDENS. On this Centre Island central corridor, you'll find an island centrepiece, a hedge maze, a reflecting pool, a fountain and colourful plantings. Bike and boat rentals are nearby.

CENTREVILLE AMUSEMENT PARK. Light-weight reasonably-priced rides for the kids. Try the antique carousel and the train.

FAR ENOUGH FARM. A petting farm for kids up to 12 years old.

GIBRALTAR POINT CENTRE FOR THE ARTS. Housed in a former natural science school, it offers working retreat and conference facilities to visual artists. "Sound Travels" is an annual summer concert exploring electroacoustic music held at the centre.

IROQUOIS RESTAURANT: CI Food Services (9 Queens Quay, Centre Island, 203-8795).

ISLAND PARADISE RESTAURANT: CI Food Services (9 Queens Quay, Centre Island, 203-8795).

RECTORY CAFÉ (203-6011). Opposite the bridge to Algonquin Island, it's frequented by sketch artists in the summer months. Enjoy a coffee, tea and scones or why not have brunch, banana pancakes or delicious french toast? Hours vary - call ahead.

WARD'S ISLAND CAFÉ. An Island institution with great sandwiches and desserts (seasonal).

Lakefront — Heading West

Renting a bike is the best way to explore the waterfront, or don your warm parka and set out for a brisk walk among the frozen paradise of lake icicles in winter. Check the map of this section for distances and always carry enough water if you plan to walk. Public washroom facilities are located in Coronation Park east of Ontario Place.

Highlights

FORT YORK (100 Garrison Rd., 392-6907). Harbouring the largest grouping of original War of 1812 buildings, **Fort York** began as a small, palisaded garrison, built in 1793 by John Graves Simcoe to protect the entrance to what was then Toronto Harbour.

Most of the buildings date from 1813, after the original barracks and other structures were burned by U.S. troops at the Battle of York in the War of 1812. Overcoming 700 staunch defenders, 1700 US soldiers marshalled at Humber Bay Park, then overran the fort, and during six nights of terror, burned the Parliament Buildings to the ground. In retaliation, Canadian forces stormed Washington and burned down many of its public buildings, including what is now known as the White House.

This designated National Historical Site sits on 3 hectares (7 acres) of land. Gunpowder magazines, blockhouses, barracks, officers' quarters, costumed staff and period demonstrations all help breathe life into history. Open year-round, adults $5, seniors/youths $3.25, children $3.

CORONATION PARK (Lake Shore W. at Strachan, 392-1111). Find yourself in a forest-like setting here thanks to tree plantings made in honour of war veterans and conservationists, King George VI, and the countries of the British Empire. The park was created in 1934 when a seawall was built from Strachan to Bathurst. Among various military memorials and artifacts, look for the Victory Garden surrounding the tall flagpole near the sculptural circle.

SUNNYSIDE BEACHES (Martin Goodman Trail, south of High Park, 392-1111). The pedestrian boardwalk at the edge of the lake along the western beaches is made of materials recycled to look like wood planks. Take a walk along until you reach the Humber Pedestrian Bridge (see Photo section) or enjoy an ice cream from the Sunnyside Pavillion Café.

HUMBER BAY PARK (Martin Goodman Trail, at the mouth of Mimico Creek, 392-1111). A great place to view the Toronto skyline and migratory birds, the park also has a wonderful gazebo (dance with a friend!) and boardwalk.

There are also public boat launch ramps, a fully accessible fishing pier, a fly-casting pond, moorings, and model boating ponds.

At the mouth of Mimico Creek rest the two spits of land that form Humber Bay Park. Mimico, from the Indian word Omineca, means "home of the wild pigeons". Huge flocks were known to have inhabited the area at one time. Habitat restoration projects here include planting Carolinian trees and shrubs, establishing wildflower meadows, and providing a warm water fish habitat and wetland on the east peninsula.

The shores of Humber Bay are a natural purification plant as storm water runoff is collected and directed into a multi-celled treatment basin and wetland complex, purifying it before the water is returned to Lake Ontario.

COLONEL SAMUEL SMITH PARK (Lakeshore Blvd. W. between 13th and 23rd Sts., 392-1111). This park is a naturalist's dream. Hiking trails lead through extensive mature forest wetlands habitat, and down to Lake Ontario (see Photo section). Fish spawn in the offshore rocks, and turtles pop their heads up on nearby islands. You can visit a snake hibernation and basking area in the created wetland habitat. The park is also growing in popularity with migrating birds (over 200 species have been catalogued).

Recently, a small boat basin was created as part of a lakefill project. The surrounding habitats include meadows, mud flats, seasonally inundated flood flats, amphibian ponds and shorebird habitation. In all, this exquisite park, painstakingly reclaimed, covers over 10 hectares of the waterfront.

MARIE CURTIS PARK (Waterfront Trail and Etobicoke Creek, 392-1111). Marie Curtis was a major mover and shaker in the formation of a regional parkland system when she was a member of the first Metro Toronto Council back in 1954. Marie Curtis Park wraps around the Etobicoke Creek as it flows into Lake Ontario. Devastated by Hurricane Hazel's floodwaters in 1954, the floodplain became a marsh habitat for waterfowl. A pedestrian bridge over the marsch links the east and west banks of the creek, offering a lovely look-out point. Alderwood Interpretive Trail follows Etobicoke Creek above Lake Shore Blvd W. and there's a supervised swimming beach there in July and August.

Things to Do, See, Buy & Eat

OLD GARRISON BURYING GROUND (Portland at Wellington). This is the oldest European burying ground in Toronto, featuring a monument honouring the military dead from the battle of York.

EXHIBITION PLACE. Main entrances at Dufferin and Gardiner Expwy/Bathurst and Lakeshore Blvd. Features include a rose garden and a peace monument overlooking the lakeshore.

WATERFRONT

THE NATIONAL TRADE CENTRE (NTC) (Exhibition Place, 263-3000). Opened in 1997, the NTC offers a variety of services to the international trade show industry, delegates and to the regional and local community. "Shoreline", one of the 3 public art commissions at the NTC, consists of 135,000 individually laid paving stones. The wave patterns this created is expressed by the artist Jerry Clapsaddle as a metaphor for the flow of trade as well as the forces of nature on the site.

CANADIAN NATIONAL EXHIBITION (CNE) (393-6300). Beyond traditional fair rides and games, you can also find horticultural, livestock, entertainment and cultural events at this longstanding Toronto fairground. Every year since 1878, late August has meant it's time for Canadians to descend on the fair to partake in Toronto's Exhibition tradition. The Royal Winter (agricultural) Fair is also held on the grounds in November.

ONTARIO PLACE/ CINESPHERE (955 Lake Shore Blvd. W., 314-9900). Home of the first Imax theatre, this entertainment and leisure haven includes the Molson Amphitheatre which features live concerts (870-8000), a marina, the Imax Theatre, a water slide and the H.M.S. Haida (WWII destroyer open for tours). The Imax Theatre often shows nature and ecology films, so be sure to check the schedule for an experience as close to nature as you can get without being in it.

MARILYN BELL PARK (Aquatic Dr. and Lakeshore Blvd). Named for the first person to swim Lake Ontario, it is accessed by a pedestrian bridge across Lake Shore Blvd.

SUNNYSIDE POOL (1755 Lakeshore Blvd. W., 392-1111). Opened June 28, 1922, it displays great art-deco design. Swim and enjoy the architecture at the same time.

SUNNYSIDE CAFÉ (1755 Lakeshore Blvd. W. at Sunnyside Pavillion, 531-2233). In addition to a café they do continuous work to keep the western beaches and tunnel clean.

CLIFF LUMSDEN PARK (Lakeshore Dr. and 5th St.). Named for internationally known Canadian swimmer from the 50s, it offers a dramatic vista of Lake Ontario.

R. L. CLARK FILTRATION PLANT. At the foot of 23rd Landscaped grounds and a park-like setting. One of four major filtration plants that has a 1,365 megalitre filtering capacity.

SOUTH ETOBICOKE REGENERATION PROJECT (503-9826). An active forum of local businesses, concerned citizens, environmentalists and educational institutions co-operating to revitalize this lakeshore district.

Lakefront — Heading East

Highlights

TOMMY THOMPSON PARK ("LESLIE STREET SPIT") (Leslie and Lakeshore Blvd. E., 661-6600). Want to visit the home of rare plants, uncommon birds, and creatures large and small? Don't miss North America's most remarkable urban wilderness park.

Close to 400 rare plant species have been identified here. These include prickly pear cactus, ladies' tresses, bog twayblade, asters, and numerous species of grasses. Nearly 300 species of birds, both migratory and breeding, have been sighted (even more than in Algonquin Park). Sightings include double-breasted cormorants, caspian terns, snowy owls, and many species of ducks and shorebirds. Melanistic (black) garter snakes, a rare mutation of the common garter snake, turtles and several species of frogs also make "The Spit" their home. In addition to small creatures like voles and mice, larger animals, including beavers, otters, red foxes, and coyotes have been sighted.

Leslie Spit has the largest inland seagull colony in North America — it's home to 40 to 50 thousand ring-billed gulls. You can even see beavers here if you are lucky! 22

From entrance gate to tip, this spit of land juts 5 kilometres into Lake Ontario near the harbour's eastern entrance. Built forty years ago as breakwater protection for harbour expansion, it was called the Leslie Spit (as many locals still refer to it). But the harbour never expanded. Over 4 million truckloads of fill from development sites and dredged material from the outer harbour sat untouched.

Today, it has been transformed by nature into an extraordinary wildlife preserve. A car-free refuge from the hustle and bustle of the city, it makes for an ideal breather amid flora and fauna friends. Tommy Thompson, the park's namesake, was well known for the invitation to 'please walk on the grass' posted far and wide in city parks.

Due to the environmental sensitivity of the spit, access is closely regulated. Because of the spit's length, the best way to explore is by bike. Rent a bike from Harbourfront or take the TTC. A shuttle bus occasionally runs between the streetcar stop and into the park on weekends for walkers. The park is not open to motor vehicles. Open weekends. For more information, including Sunday summer tours, call 661-6600.

WATERFRONT

Friends of the Spit is an advocacy group dedicated to keeping the Leslie Spit a car-free environmental resource that is entirely public, accessible, and free. For more info on preservation of the Spit, call 699-3143 or visit www.interlog.com/~fos.

The Beaches

From Kingston Rd. down to the lake between Woodbine and Victoria Park Aves.

The Essence

Whether you have a few hours or a few days, at any time of year the Beaches area offers something for everyone. It has a wonderful feel to it — outdoor living.

You can get here along Queen E, but the Martin Goodman Trail will bring you here as well. This is a kids and dogs kind of place specializing in simple pleasures. Peaceful walks in beautiful gardens are steps away from boisterous sessions of beach volleyball. Contentedly bask in the sun, amble along the three-kilometre boardwalk or try some in-line skating. Listen to jazz, do some shopping or just watch the world pass by at a funky cafe. You might find musicians playing or a local arts and crafts show in one of the many community parks.

Wander the side streets where hundred-year-old Queen Anne style homes rub shoulders with their architecturally cutting-edge neighbours. When winter hits, skate at an outdoor rink, sip hot chocolate at a cozy café, or admire the lake during a bracing boardwalk stroll.

The boardwalk fronts the beach and runs about three kilometres along the waterfront. Parks, snack shops and fast food places sit right along the Martin Goodman trail. Joggers, bikers, and in-line skaters are out day and night breezing past tennis courts, lawn bowling and lacrosse fields. At the western end of the boardwalk, consider a dip in the Donald D. Summerville pool. Lifeguards staff the beach during the summer, and daily postings alert visitors to water quality, temperature, and safe swimming times.

On Queen at Glen Manor, noise dies down as you enter Glen Stewart Ravine. Shaded and cool on even the hottest summer days, you can unwind amid the many rare native plant species, and saunter the banks of one of the few remaining natural streams in the city. Wherever you turn, it's clear that this is a neighbourhood sensitive to its multi-faceted heritage.

The Eastern Ravine and Beaches Discovery Walk self-guided tour will give you a feel for all that this neighbourhood has to offer. (See page 118.)

Ponder the stars at night from the beach.

The Roots — A Taste of History

Philadelphia's Ashbridge family established themselves at the western edge of today's community in the 1790s. They and a few others farmed the district until the late 1800s. In 1853, to their east, Joseph Williams built his home, Kew Farm. In the early 1900s it became Kew Gardens, and along with Ashbridge's Bay Park, shared the waterfront stretch with Woodbine, Scarborough, Balmy, and Victoria Park beaches.

Moving into the twentieth century, folk from nearby Toronto discovered this convenient summer escape from the sweltering heat and press of city life. In the 1880s, a tramline delivered hundreds of revellers from town each weekend. Where at first they came to picnic and play, they later built their kiosks and cottages. The chain of sandy beaches became Toronto's Lido.

By the 1920s, a Toronto hungry for land lurched eastward. New homes sprang up, cottages were winterized, and the playground came of age as a year- round community. The Beaches never lost its casual, get-away style and entered the twenty-first century as a most popular active living neighbourhood. Offbeat shops along Queen, many displaying the work of local artists and artisans, help give the neighbourhood a distinct and artsy character.

In Glen Stewart Ravine, migratory birds rest among artifacts dating back some 4,000 years. [23]

Highlights

EASTERN RAVINES & BEACHES DISCOVERY WALK. The recommended starting point for this walk is at the north end of the Glen Stewart Ravine on the south side of Kingston Rd., east of Main Street. From here you make your way to the lakefront in about 30 minutes of woodland stroll. It's easy to spend a whole day here, but the beach awaits. When you hit the boardwalk, you have to choose whether to head east or west (the lake is to the south of the boardwalk).

Choose to walk east and you head towards the R. C. Harris Filtration Plant (see below). This walk has a strong neighbourhood feel to it. Many of the streets come right down to the boardwalk, and just before the filtration plant, they seem to vanish into the sand.

Strike out west and you head in the direction of Summerville swimming pool, Ashbridge's Bay Park, and the conclusion of the walk at Coxwell and Queen. Call 392-1111 for details.

In Spring, 2001 the first working wind turbine in a North American city (near Ashbridge's Bay Treatment plant) will produce non polluting power. One windmill can power approximately 300–500 individual households. Call TREC for info (see Resource Groups page 151). [24]

R. C. HARRIS FILTRATION PLANT (2701 Queen E., 392-3566 for tours). This art deco stunner spans several acres at the bottom of Victoria Park Ave. (see Photo section). Built in the 1930s, the plant has been declared a National Historic Civil Engineering Site. More than just a pretty water filtration plant, the south eastern point of the property offers the only good view of the Scarborough Bluffs (see page 120) visible from the Beaches. It is Toronto's largest water treatment facility, producing water to meet 47 per cent of

Toronto's and Region of York's water requirements. As more than five million people get their drinking water from Lake Ontario, this is one of four filtration plants required to treat over 2,300 million litres per day. It's surrounded by a large park with rolling lawns and spectacular views. For more info and depth, there are free guided tours on Saturdays.

KEW GARDENS (Lee at Queen). This broad, manicured park is the site of fairs and concerts throughout the year and a great place for a game of baseball, a picnic or a concert at the open air gazebo in summer. It has beautiful gardens, room to spare, and lots of shade. The Kew Beach War Memorial is the park's official gateway and honours those who served during both World Wars.

ASHBRIDGE'S BAY PARK (Lakeshore Blvd. E., east of Coxwell). You'd never guess that this well-kept beach was created from excavation site landfill. Ashbridge's Bay originally included the marshlands to the west, but over time, the marshes were filled in and given over to industrial use.

These days it's anything but industrial. Kids spend hours by the shore filling their sand buckets or clamouring over the assortment of huge rocks. Sporty types take advantage of the rugby pitch and slow pitch softball diamonds. Boating types use the launch ramps, marinas and moorings to fuel their nautical passions. And if you dig archaeology, ask about the important and exciting discoveries being made nearby. Conveniently, the Martin Goodman Trail meets the Beaches Boardwalk at the north end of the park.

Things to Do, See, Buy & Eat

WOODBINE PARK. On the site of Toronto's historic Greenwood Racetrack, there is now a 12 hectare (30-acre) community park. Look for the bronzed tree among its growing arboreal neighbours together forming the "circle of trees".

THE BEACHES BOARDWALK. Don't miss a stroll along the shoreline. You can get to the Eastern Beaches Discovery Walk from here.

THE BEACH. Don't miss relaxing in the sun by the lake, hearing the waves crash on the shore and people watching!

ECOWORKS (24 Cummings, 461-6121). Make an appointment to stop by and check out this innovative planet-friendly gift service.

VELOTIQUE LTD. (592 Queen E., 466-3171). Bike clothing and accessories.

STREETCITY BIKES (1178 Queen E., 466-7492). Bikes for sale, rentals and more!

MOOSE CROSSING CRAFT GALLERY (1834 Queen E., 694-0233). Crafts and gallery that celebrate the use of recycled materials.

THE BODY SHOP (1925 Queen E., 694-9936). Cosmetics and body care that also cares for the environment. Many locations throughout Toronto.

JAMAICA SUNRISE (1959 Queen E., 691-2999). Jamaican delights for all palates.

PLANET SKATE (2144 Queen E., 690-7588). Anything from in-line skates to hockey sticks for outdoor fun.

FOX THEATRE - REPERTORY CINEMA (2236 Queen E., 691-7330). The oldest continually running movie house in Toronto.

Scarborough Bluffs

SCARBOROUGH BLUFFS / BLUFFER'S PARK (Brimley Rd. and Lake Ontario, 392-8186). If you continue east you'll encounter the Bluffs, a Scarborough landmark. Including twists and turns, the Bluffs are about eight kilometres from the Beaches area. They deserve a visit, but you might want to plan this as a special outing. (See Photo section.)

The Bluffs are a centrefold spread of the geological record, a snapshot in time of the last ice age. The various strata describe the ebb and flow of ice sheets as well as the deposits of long vanished glacial lakes. Now the park sits on 2.6 million cubic metres of landfill, mostly from the excavation of the Bloor subway line.

Elizabeth, wife of John Graves Simcoe, named the Scarborough Bluffs as their boat passed by on their first trip to the town of York. On first glimpse she was reminded of the cliffs near her own home, Scarborough in England. In commemoration, she gave these bluffs the same name.

Also worth visiting:

MURAL ROUTES (1859 Kingston Rd., 698-7322). Outdoor art gallery of 12 historic murals along Kingston Rd.
ROSETTA McCLAIN GARDENS (Kingston Rd. & Glen Everest Rd., 392-8186). Magnificent bluff-top view, accessible, with mature trees, limestone rockery, pet cemetery and formal gardens that include plants with distinctive fragrances for heightened appreciation of the visually impaired.
SCARBOROUGH ARTS COUNCIL (1859 Kingston Rd., 698-7322). Encouraging development of the arts in Scarborough.
BLUFFS GALLERY (1959 Kingston Rd., inside Scarborough Arts Council, 691-7322). Fine arts and crafts.

THE VERTICALS

Now that we've covered the downtown core, the waterfront and the Toronto Islands, it's time to explore the verticals taking us north in the city. To stay with a water focus, we begin with the Humber and Don Rivers — Toronto's two main river ravines. Next we take you from where we left off at Bloor and explore Yonge north.

The Humber River

The Essence

On the west side of town, you can follow the Humber River from Lake Ontario northwards for more than 27 kilometres (17 miles) to the top of Toronto and for many miles more on its way out of town. The farther away you get from the Lake, the more the welter of tributaries makes the Humber increasingly difficult to follow. You could never do the whole thing in one day, but the good news is that wherever you end up, you're sure to find something good.

The Humber River watershed covers 857 square kilometres (343 sq miles) making it the largest watershed

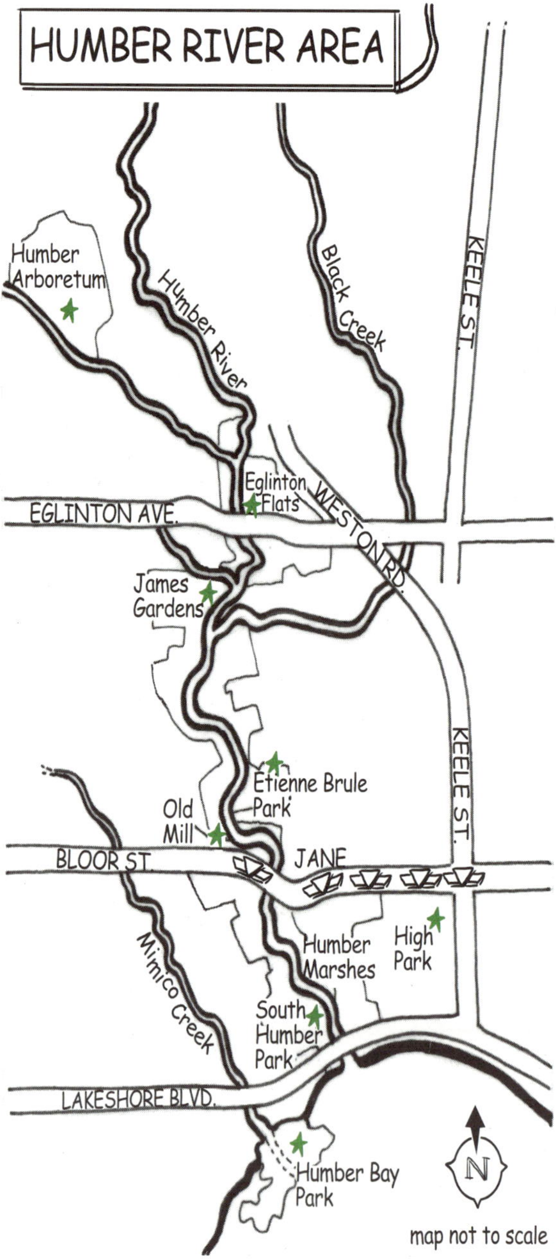
HUMBER RIVER AREA
Humber Arboretum
Humber River
Black Creek
KEELE ST.
Eglinton Flats
EGLINTON AVE.
WESTON RD.
James Gardens
Etienne Brule Park
Old Mill
BLOOR ST.
JANE
KEELE ST.
Humber Marshes
High Park
Mimico Creek
South Humber Park
LAKESHORE BLVD.
Humber Bay Park
N
map not to scale

in the Toronto region. Our guidebook trip along the Humber is really an exploration of some of the highlights of the Humber River Valley. And we won't get to everything. We can tell you, though, that the bird-watching is great, the plant and wildlife species are plentiful, and the trails and paths are well marked and safe.

But if you have a special interest in birding, for example, you will want to check out our Resource Groups (see page 151) to find the experts. A most important thing to remember is that each season has something on offer, making the Humber River an uncontested highlight in any visit to Toronto.

The Roots — A Taste of History

If you were a pioneer looking for a place to start a new life, you would want to make sure you had access to an abundance of food and fresh water. You would not want to be cut off from the little civilization available, but would want enough space to meet present and future needs. You would be sorely tempted to set up housekeeping along the Humber River. And the earliest European settlers, the French, did just that.

The Humber was the hinterland's version of Main Street. Flowing from the Oak Ridges Moraine at the Niagara Escarpment, its course was sculpted over thousands of years. Before the arrival of explorers, Canada's native people eased the burdens of trade and travel with a stitch-work of trails that knit region to region and culture to culture.

Copper, tobacco, fishnets and furs moved from areas of supply to areas of demand. Hunters found the fish and game that meant survival. Warriors sped to the battlefields. Messengers made their way from village to village.

Winding up the Humber Valley from marshy river mouth to life-giving moraine north of Toronto, and then via a short portage to the Holland River and Lake Simcoe, The Toronto Carrying Place Trail linked the Lake Ontario region with the Upper Great Lakes. It stood as a symbol of the interaction among people, land and water. By the late 1700s, surveyors included the Toronto Carrying Place as 'Old Indian Trail' on area surveys. The earliest settlements used the Trail as their road until grid-type replacements were cut through the bush.

John Graves Simcoe, first Lieutenant-Governor of Upper Canda, considered using the trail as a military road to the north, but instead chose to build Canada's longest thoroughfare, Yonge Street.

In 1954, Hurricane Hazel, the worst storm in Toronto's history, ravaged the city and hit the Humber Valley area particularly hard. The watershed's huge flood plain was inundated at a cost of losses in lives and property. To prevent similar disasters, the City of Toronto has taken over much of the land associated with the flood plain. The early response was to seek ways to control the river and its tributaries. In many cases, this meant interfering with the watercourses through channelling and damming. While an immediate and at the time necessary solution, it has had damaging long term consequences.

Natural habitat was destroyed and the waters became polluted. Recently, the concrete channels and dams have begun to crumble. Community groups like the Black Creek Project, Friends of Mimico Creek, and the Action to Restore a Clean Humber have joined forces with the City of Toronto and the Toronto and Region Conservation Authority (TRCA) and other government agencies to restore the health of the Humber River and Etobicoke and Mimico Creeks (see Resource Groups page 151). An official plan called *Legacy: A Strategy for a Healthy Humber*, was approved by the Toronto Region and Conservation Authority and will guide those protecting and preserving the watershed.

Activities to reclaim the Humber are varied. In a unique treatment process, the ponds of a recently built park complex filter sediment from water before returning it to the river. Fishways that allow migratory species to safely pass around or over river barriers are helping to replenish vanishing stocks. Concrete channel embankments are being removed and recycled so that watercourses can find their way back to long lost beds. Plans to restore much of the marshland habitat at the river's mouth will ensure that vulnerable plant and animal life survive.

The corridors of the Humber are critical to the survival of rare and endangered plant and wild life in Toronto. Brook Trout can flourish in its cold waters. Red-shouldered Hawks soar over high quality forest and wetlands. More than 1,000 kinds of plants are found along the Humber including raspberries, ostrich ferns, dogwoods, and sunflower. The Humber holds the archaeological and geological record of an evolving land mass, and bears witness to an ever-changing landscape. It is a place to play of unique and remarkable character, as well as a scientific microcosm drawing attention from around the globe.

On the morning of September 24, 1999 as the rising sun burned off the dawn mists in Etienne Brulé Park, a First Nations Community Sunrise Ceremony marked the day the Humber was designated a Canadian Heritage River by the Canadian government. As the twenty-sixth Canadian river so named, the Humber was recognized for its outstanding human heritage and recreational values, along with the contribution it has made to the development of the country. Thus protected, it will endure to teach and enchant generations to come.

Humber River

Highlights

HUMBER VALLEY TRAIL. The Humber's first trappers, traders, and travellers used the Toronto Carrying Place Trail. Today, cyclists, hikers, and in-line skaters have the Humber Valley Trail. Winding out of the Martin Goodman Trail at the Humber's mouth, it follows a serpentine course north for 10.5 kilometres (6.5 miles) past formal gardens and through woods, ravines, meadows and marshlands to Raymore Park, just south of Lawrence. We're going to cover the trail as far north as James Gardens including some of the highlights along the way.

But you can take a stroll or bike up the five kilometres from Bloor to Eglinton (Rent a bike on Bloor at Jane if you choose to ride). Access is from Bloor (Old Mill subway).

HUMBER RIVER, OLD MILL & MARSHES DISCOVERY WALK. With a Discovery Walk route map (see page 35) in hand, you can trek from Lake Ontario to Bloor and take in (along with the river, the mill and the marshes) the Old Mill Bridge, a portion of the ancient Toronto Carrying Place Trail, and the site of an early settlement and nearby Rousseaux trading post. Call 392-1111 for details.

More than 60 species of fish live in the Humber River, including salmon, pike and trout. [25]

SOUTH HUMBER PARK (Stephen Dr., north of The Queensway, 392-1111). Have a look at the nationally rare species of white sassafras found in an immature red oak forest. Or cross the Humber Pedestrian Bridge (see Photo section) built in 1994 to span the mouth of the Humber River and connect the Waterfront/Martin Goodman Trail with the Humber Valley Trail. The bridge won design awards for its aboriginal and historical motifs.

HUMBER MARSHES (West bank, north of The Queensway Bridge, 392-1111). An area undergoing substantial rejuvenation, the Humber Marsh supports more than 120 types of plants and as many different kinds of birds. The marsh's ecosystem is pretty well intact and goes back thousands of years.

The Tree Advocate planting program has been a major environmental initiative to improve the urban forest in the City and identify new tree-planting locations. The goal: to plant 60,000 native trees on city owned land over the year 2000. [26]

KING'S MILL PARK (Glenaden Ave. E. at Prince Edward Dr. S., 392-1111). One of the first area mills was built here in 1793, supplying wood for the construction of **Fort York**. See the ruins of the "Old Mill", its third and final incarnation. A bridge has spanned the Humber at this point since 1837. The existing Old Mill Bridge was built in 1917 to replace a wooden one destroyed by ice. Further along you will round a bend taking you past an old Iroquois Village, Taieigon, where explorers Cavalier de la Salle and Fathers Hennepin and La Motte stayed.

ÉTIENNE BRULÉ PARK (Old Mill Rd. at Lundy, on the east side of the river, 392-1111). Paddle in the pool during summer, indulge in some seasonal fishing or take the kids to the playground. And in winter? If you love cross-country skiing — you're home. Etienne Brulé is believed to be the first European to see Lake Ontario, during his travels in 1615. Look for the commemorative plaque and marker paying tribute to Brulé's adventurous journey.

HOME SMITH PARK (Old Dundas and Old Mill, on the west side of the Humber River, 392-1111). This park is picnic central in the area. In 1994, the Boy Scouts of Canada planted over 4,000 cedar and sugar maple tree seedlings here. There is also a mature sugar maple stand in the northern part of the park. The area commemorates community development in the Humber Valley in the early 1900's by developer Robert Home Smith.

LAMBTON WOODS PARK (Edenbridge at Royal York Rd., 392-1111). The Village of Lambton Mills, a major 19th century community at the crossing of the Humber River and Dundas W. gave its name to the park. Today you will find valley wilderness and nature trails rich in plant life and a wildflower preserve near James Gardens. The historic Lambton Hotel (4066 Old Dundas) survives to this day, restored as a community and heritage centre.

JAMES GARDENS (Edenbridge close to Eglinton on the west side, 392-8186). James Gardens is a seductive oasis, and your best view of the Gardens is offered from the lookout platform next to the James house. As you saunter amidst the shrubbery, look for such uncommon tree species as Dawn Redwood and Redbud. The lush green of its natural carpet, the plumage of ferns, an elegant gazebo, and graceful bridges all invite you to linger. Towering maple, willow and spruce trees promise well-shaded intimacy. A trail winding south along a small stream enters Lambton Woods, valued for its Trillium, Trip Willie, Hepatica and others.

Many wedding photos are taken here, and it is not unusual to see movie crews filming. Should you tire, there are picnic facilities and water fountains along the path.

EGLINTON FLATS (Eglinton and Jane, 392-1111).This concentrated park is a great find for anyone with an archaeological interest (or a kite). There are still aspects that are unexplored. It is suspected that sites here are layered. Although it is modified, landscaped and planted, you can still get a sense of a green area that is close to its natural state. The park also offers lacrosse and soccer fields, a public golf course, tennis courts and a secluded area for open air theatre.

Things to Do, See, Buy & Eat

LAMBTON HOUSE (4066 Old Dundas W., 767-5472). The last remaining landmark on the east side of the Humber River from the Lambton Mills period, this first restoration project of Heritage York was built in 1847.

CALATRAVA BRIDGE (1 km west of Humber River). A bridge whose creation allowed the restoration of Mimico Creek's mouth with native plants, including a huge patch of spring blooming iris.

PORTFOOLIO ART AND CRAFT GALLERY (4196 Dundas W., 236-9156). Offers many artists demos (painting, glass, ceramics, woodworking and metal).

Why not fly a kite today?

The Don River

The Essence

The Don River is intimately connected to the life of our city. One of the most urbanized watersheds in Canada, it holds approximately 2,500 people for each kilometre of river. From Lake Ontario at the Keating Channel, it cuts almost directly through the heart of town, its tendrils snaking north for 38 kilometres (24 miles), its valley etching a course for prime city parkland.

At the Forks of the Don, barely a third of its way through Toronto from Lake Ontario, the river splits dramatically into three, reaching far to the east, north and north west. It's an ambitious undertaking, but if you allow a few days, you can follow well-tended trails almost anywhere along its many tributaries. At stops along the way, you can examine the geological record of Toronto since the last ice age, explore some of the naturalization projects that are returning the valley to good environmental health, and learn more about Toronto's history. Best of all, you can escape from the city's nerve centre to ravine peace and quiet without leaving town.

Including all its tributaries, the Don watershed covers 370 square kilometres (148 sq miles). In 1950, it was declared the most polluted river in Canada but thanks to incredible citizen and city efforts, it is getting cleaner all the time. Cleaning up the Don is estimated to cost more than $1 billion overall, at the rate of approximately $30 to $60 million a year.

The Roots — A Taste of History

Throughout the early 1700s, some 40 grist, lumber, paper and flour mills force-fed the river their leftovers. Each new industry followed that lead. For most of modern times, a looming confusion of residential, business and industrial encampments along its edge have threatened the health of the river. Blanketed with landfill, the marshland ceased to exist. In its place, new port structures sprang up along an equally new shoreline.

Toronto bracketed the Lower Don with two major roadways: the Bayview Extension and the Don Valley Parkway. Only eight kilometres long, this section flows through steep valley walls rimmed by some of the city's most developed and densely populated neighbourhoods. Straightened to suffer the constraints of cement-walled channels, even the river's mouth has been right-angled at the Keating Channel.

The upper reaches of this river system fared better, but not well. Dammed, channelled and redirected to control downstream flooding and harness power, they too became repositories for industrial and urban detritus. Fish and wildlife all but disappeared, and without help, they will never return to their former numbers.

Reclamation efforts are well underway. Concentrated planting efforts have introduced more than 35,000 trees and shrubs and thousands of wildflowers to the Lower Don.

Another main effort, the "Elevated Wetlands" (www.elevatedwetlands.com), includes a temporarily functioning wetland sculpture. Visible through the car window from the Don Valley Parkway, these tooth-like structures draw attention to the importance of wetlands as an ecosystem. Water is drawn from the Don River into the elevated area where wetland plants and trees naturally remove pollutants from the water before sending it back through a series of wetlands to the Don River.

The Chester Springs Marsh (see page 131) is another main focus. It is being nurtured as a wetland that provides critical urban wildlife habitat. Planting alone isn't enough though, and clean-up activities are just as important. The work to be done will require another two generations of people who care before it is complete.

More than 800,000 people live in the watershed's 370 square kilometres (148 sq miles), making it our most urban river. The Don River is tied to our history, bound to our present and linked the health of our future.

DON RIVER AREA
Earl Bales Park
HWY 401
Betty Sutherland Park
YORK MILLS
Edwards Gardens
Sunnybrook Park
Sherwood Park
EGLINTON AVE.
Ontario Science Centre
E.T. Seton Park
ST CLAIR
O'CONNOR
Don Valley Brickworks
Todmorden Mills Park
BLOOR
DANFORTH AVE.
Toronto Necropolis
Riverdale Farm and Park
YONGE ST.
N
map not to scale
Ashbridge's Bay Park
Tommy Thompson Park/ Leslie Spit

Lower Don River

From Lake Ontario to the forks of the Don.

Highlights

DON VALLEY HILLS AND DALES DISCOVERY WALK. If you want to satisfy that get-out-of-town feeling, this is your chance. The trails on this walk cover the area from Riverdale Farm (see page 76) in the south to Todmorden Mills (see below) at the top. It's easy to get to using public transit. On the way, you will explore the paths of the Toronto Necropolis (see page 76), walk the banks of the Don River through Chester Springs Marsh (see below) and pass under the Prince Edward Viaduct (see page 101). You should allow at least three hours to walk the route, and more if you pause along the way. Call 392-1111 for details.

Over 21 million people visit Toronto each year. Imagine the impacts! Imagine the greening opportunities! [27]

CHESTER SPRINGS MARSH (East side of the Don River, south of the Bloor Viaduct, 392-1111). One of many revitalization projects on the Don River, this one was initiated to recreate a wetland environment. Now, thanks to the tireless efforts of volunteer clean-up crews, planters, and custodians, it is home to the herons, turtles, and red foxes that had all but vanished from the Don Valley. Interpretive signage and brochures are available to help visitors fathom the miraculous reclamation of a once-desolate location.

TODMORDEN MILLS (Pottery Rd. west of Broadview, 396-2819). Step into Don Valley history, and see how a wildflower preserve is helping to return a degraded natural area to vibrant good health. The wildflower preserve covers nearly 10 hectares (23 acres) of land around Todmorden Mills. It offers six habitat types, a U-shaped oxbow marking part of the original course of the Don River, and "Tod Mountain", that was made from the excavated fill of 1960s skyscrapers. The mill is also a great place for a picnic and links various pedestrian and bicycle trails. Walk north from Broadview subway to Pottery Rd and then walk downhill.

When Thomas Helliwell left Yorkshire for Toronto in 1820, he chose 4 hectares (10 acres) of the Don Valley on which to build his home and his brewery, malt house and distillery. On your visit you can see five structures, including a paper mill, brewery, the picture book Don Railway Station, and two homes, all representing life in the early 1800s.

Use a bike or in-line skates to get up the Don Trail. It is also accessible by TTC. Call 393-INFO.

DON VALLEY BRICK WORKS (At the Forks of the Don River, 392-1111). Nowhere else in town will you find a remnant of Toronto's industrial past, combined with an awe-inspiring representation of its geological and fossil record and a striking cross-section of its natural heritage - all in one award-winning, internationally-famous public park. (See Photo section.)

The north slope of the Brick Works stands some 25 metres over the exposed Georgian Bay Shale at the base of the pit. Rising above the shale, the various tills, formations, clays and terraces record the ebb and flow of massive sheets of ice whose slow, irresistible rhythm marked time as the continent shifted and evolved.

On its way from the area of the former Downsview Airport, Mud Creek was altered and diverted into an underground tunnel to carry storm water drainage. Factory waste, agricultural runoff, and other urban abuses have seriously upset the ecological balance. Where it enters this park, the creek mixes with groundwater, providing water needed to create new wetland habitats. The water resides in the wetland ponds of the quarry gardens where it undergoes natural filtering before emptying into the Don River.

While you're here, visit the gardens, wetlands, and wildflower meadows. The meadows in particular contain grasses representing 70% of the types found in many old field meadows of Southern Ontario. Flowering plants include black-eyed susan, bergamot, evening primrose, aster, and goldenrod. Wetter zones have plants like great lobelia, notting nurr-marigold, swamp milkweed and marsh marigold. The colour and brilliance of these fields on a warm summer's day are alone worth the trip. And there's more.

A mural painted by artist Sady Ducros in 1996 (88 metres long and about 5 metres high or 293 by 16 feet) is located on the building furthest to the north east, which you can see from the road. It celebrates the themes of geology, natural and industrial history, and regeneration. From the left side, geology gives way to native plant and animal species over the ages, followed by brick making, both as a process and as an influence in Toronto architecture.

Things to Do, See, Buy & Eat

ST. JAMES CEMETERY (Parliament and Bloor E., 964-9194). Incredible design, materials, and execution. Woodland environments and ravine vistas make for a quietly refreshing summer or winter walk (circa 1845).
EAST SIDE PLAYERS (75 Fairfield Rd., 425 0917). For local theatre productions.

Toronto's Blue Box Recycling Program diverted 130,500 tonnes of garbage from landfill in 1998. [28]

North-West from the Forks of the Don

Highlights

ERNEST THOMPSON SETON PARK (Leslie and Don Mills, north of Eglinton, 392-1111). Along with great picnic possibilities, this park summons the traveller to enjoy its archery range, equestrian trail and swimming pool. Seton was an outstanding naturalist. His concept of bringing boys together to study and enjoy the wild was later adopted by Lord Baden-Powell, who founded the Boy Scouts.
ONTARIO SCIENCE CENTRE & OMNIMAX (770 Don Mills, 696-1000). Learn about the earth's ecosystem and atmosphere in a hands-on exhibit called 'The Living Earth'. You could spend a hour or two or a whole day here. Even after a full day, you won't see everything and you may not want to leave. In addition to self-guided exploration, there are classes, demonstrations, and a variety of programs that run throughout the year. More than 800 exhibits fill the 13 halls. Tours into the Don River area are also offered from here.

The Centre houses its own Imax screen in the Omnimax Theatre. Shooting the rapids, plunging deep into the Grand Canyon in a small plane, or plummeting from the heights on the world's tallest roller coaster, you will have to pry your fingers from the arm rests, so real is the sensation. Adults $12, seniors/youth $7, children $6.
SUNNYBROOK PARK (Eglinton and Leslie, north east corner, 392-1111). The Toronto Field Naturalists opened the first urban wilderness trail in Canada here in

1930, and to this day operate an information centre in a log cabin near the entrance gates. Horseback riding is available at the Central Don Stables. Heavily treed forest areas, featuring mature sugar maples and eastern hemlock offer shaded escape on a hot summer's day. Adjacent to Sunnybrook is Serena Gundy Park at Leslie and Eglinton Avenue. This park was donated by the Gundy Estate in 1960, on the condition that $200,000 would be spent over 10 years for park improvements.

Edwards Gardens

EDWARDS GARDENS & CIVIC GARDEN CENTRE (777 Lawrence E., 397-1340). Carefully cultivated garden areas, intimate glades and wide and winding paths seem custom made for photographic magic. Nestled along the Wilket Creek ravine, you'll find a mix of planned gardens, topiary, and parkland woven together. The creek has been carefully dammed to provide a series of reflecting pools and small waterfalls. Black walnut, maple and oak trees dominate the ravines, completing the transition from carefully manicured formality to rustic wooded paths. Check out the Civic Garden Centre that hosts numerous workshops, tours and other public events year-round.

The 3 best spring blossom viewing places in the City are: Edwards Gardens, High Park, and Alexander Muir Gardens. 29

Central Don River Valley

Highlights

CHARLES SAURIOL CONSERVATION RESERVE (From the Forks of the Don to Eglinton E, 392-1111). Established in 1991, the reserve recognizes the conservation efforts of Charles Sauriol, who died that same year. Author, local resident and ardent naturalist, Sauriol was committed to protecting the Don habitat. A prolific writer, he authored several books and numerous articles detailing his life spent trekking through the Don Valley. He is also credited with the establishment of the conservation movement in Toronto.

TAYLOR CREEK & PARK (Enter by Don Mills, Haldon or Dawes Rd, 392-1111). Extending east along Taylor Creek from the Forks of the Don, this park meanders for kilometres along the course of one of the Don's major tributaries. Fitness trails, picnic and fire pit areas, lots of wildlife amid mature forest, scrub, and marsh habitats are all features of the park. The trails are well marked and there are lots of interesting side trips that bring you out of the bush and into the various neighbourhoods north of Danforth.

The watercourse is also known as Massey Creek and was originally called Silver Creek, but it has gone by several names largely due to inhabitants along its length christening it whenever a local notable caught their imagination.

There are numerous pedestrian entrances to the park along its length. Victoria Park subway is about five minutes walk from one eastern park entrance.

Yonge Street North of Bloor Street

Now back to the bustling city of buildings and culture. Yonge is the longest street in the world and a great place to begin our exploration of the city north of Bloor. From its beginning at Lake Ontario, Yonge runs over 1800 kilometres (1100 miles) to its end at Rainy River on the border between Minnesota and Ontario. Originally, it was the main road south into town. From Yonge's intersection with Steeles at the top of Toronto, the subway whisks us to the heart of town in twenty minutes. The street is a great people watching place and it is speckled with coffee shops, parkettes, trail crossings (Belt Line) and a variety of stores ranging from homeopathy to antique shops.

Yonge – St. Clair Avenue to Eglinton Avenue

Condo development is rampant in this area, as it is a liveable destination, offering parklands, trails, shops, and easy subway access. Take a while to wander along the beltline with its tiny town feel.

Highlights

CENTRAL RAVINES, BELT LINE & GARDENS DISCOVERY WALK This seven-kilometre path follows the route of Toronto's old Belt Line Railway. Join the hiking trail at **Mount Pleasant Cemetery** (see below) and go south through the Moore Park Ravine to the Don Valley Brick Works. (See page 132.)

The ravine segments of this walk are a real summer treat as they are cool, relaxing and offer an opportunity to share the experience with the racoons, chipmunks, snakes, frogs and birds. Carry on walking toward Park Drive Ravine, Vale of Avoca Ravine and pass by the front of **Mount Pleasant Cemetery**. From the cemetery, move north west to Oriole Park, then continue along the old Belt Line Railway line to complete the walk in the area of the Eglinton West subway.

MOUNT PLEASANT CEMETERY (375 Mount Pleasant Rd., at St. Clair or enter off Yonge, 485-9129). In a setting more like a park than a cemetery, celebrate the beauty permeating this historical and natural resting place. Runners and cyclists can enjoy the paths, (although dogs and in-line skaters are not permitted). Mount Pleasant was designed for people to enjoy nature in a peaceful contemplative way. The visitor finds an eye-catching landscape of gardens and trees, exquisite statuary, and overall creative, imaginative design. Because the peace here is interrupted only by quiet ceremony, they offer a safe haven to plant, animal, and bird species. More than 80 hectares (200 acres) of waterfalls, monuments, gardens, rolling hills and pathways make up this tranquil place.

Things to Do, See, Buy & Eat

XERISCAPE DEMONSTRATION GARDEN (Ministry of Environment, 135 St. Clair W.). An oasis of peace, paths with benches wind through 140 drought resistant plants and large shady trees. The garden is part of the Water Efficient Ontario Strategy which aims to hold water consumption in the province at present levels until 2011.

BELT LINE. You can access this path/park when it crosses over Yonge right near Mount Pleasant Cemetery. "Belt Line" is painted on the bridge.
TEN THOUSAND VILLAGES (2599 Yonge, 932-1673). Fairly traded handicrafts from around the world.
EGLINTON PARK HERITAGE COMMUNITY GARDEN (200 Eglinton W., behind Common Room, 781-7663). In this garden, heritage and heirloom plants of diverse origins are grown organically, and seeds are saved for the next growing season. This living gene bank preserves rare and old varieties for future generations while delighting the park's many visitors, from humans to birds and bees.
BIRDERS NATURE STORE (265 Eglinton W., 481-2431). Yard and garden décor and nature giftware.
GOVINDA'S (243 Avenue Rd., 922-5415). A vegetarian restaurant located in a Hare Krishna temple provides great northern Indian cuisine.
GARDEN AND WATERFALL OASIS. Walk past this pretty alcove garden tucked between buildings on the east side of Mt. Pleasant, south of Eglinton.
GRANITE BREWERY (245 Eglinton E., by Mount Pleasant, 322-0723). Unique brews like "Peculiar" served on an outdoor patio (all brewery spent grains are recycled to farm use).
FRAGRANT GARDEN AT CANADIAN NATIONAL INSTITUTE FOR THE BLIND (1929 Bayview, 447-5218). Garden of interesting smells, sounds and textures created by the Garden Club of Toronto.

Yonge — Lawrence Avenue To York Mills Road

Highlights

NORTHERN RAVINES & GARDENS DISCOVERY WALK (East side of Yonge and Lawrence, 392-1111). Native peoples walked these ravines as early as 4,000 years ago. They camped, hunted, and travelled through them but by the mid-1800s loggers had cut a swath through the woods. Only now are they regaining their original wilderness presence.

From just south of the Lawrence subway, you can venture forth over a mixed trail through the ravines and gullies alongside the path off Burke Brook. The current state of the brook is a testament to the damaging impact ill-considered development can have on natural

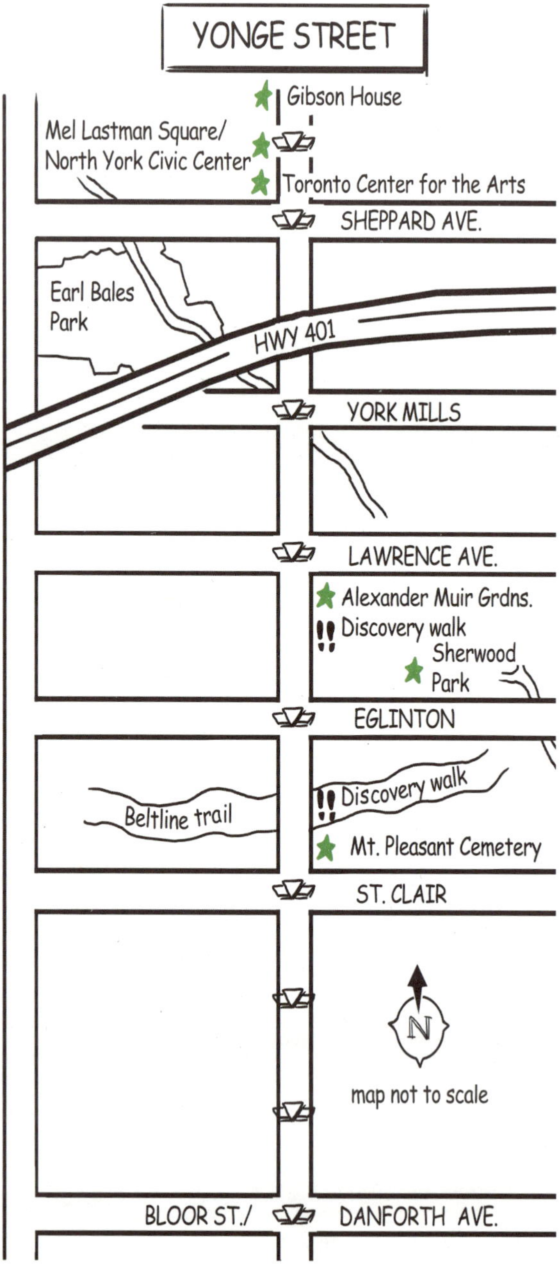
YONGE STREET
Gibson House
Mel Lastman Square/
North York Civic Center
Toronto Center for the Arts
SHEPPARD AVE.
Earl Bales
Park
HWY 401
YORK MILLS
LAWRENCE AVE.
Alexander Muir Grdns.
Discovery walk
Sherwood
Park
EGLINTON
Discovery walk
Beltline trail
Mt. Pleasant Cemetery
ST. CLAIR
N
map not to scale
BLOOR ST./
DANFORTH AVE.

resources. Fortunately, when you reach Sherwood Park Ravine, you can enjoy the Brook in its nearly untouched state. There is now an effort underway to undo the damage done when the creek was buried to allow for natural development.

Alexander Muir Memorial Gardens

Named after the composer of "The Maple Leaf Forever", Alexander Muir Memorial Gardens displays a grand achievement in the form of a multi-level planting from the 1950s that acts as a gateway into the peaceful ravine system. Then you arrive at Sherwood Park Ravine, one of the largest protected natural parks in the city. It is all that is left of the Great Lakes-St. Lawrence Forest that once covered the whole region. Some of the huge trees are at least 150 years old.

Things to Do, See, Buy & Eat

YORK MILLS VALLEY PARK (3865 Yonge, 392-8186). These flood plain lands are historically vulnerable to intense storms. Re-channelization of the river to improve drainage and control erosion was undertaken following Hurricane Hazel in 1954.

JOSEPH D. CARRIER GALLERY (901 Lawrence W., Columbus Centre, 789-7011, x 300). The gallery maintains a multicultural focus with many Italian-Canadian works and works featuring environmental themes. The community centre also has green space with picnic tables and big shady trees that are perfect for a picnic.

HERBS RESTAURANT (3187 Yonge, north of Lawrence, 322-0487). Modern French cuisine with a nutrition-conscious twist.

Yonge – Sheppard Avenue to Steeles Avenue

Highlights

TORONTO CENTRE FOR THE ARTS (5040 Yonge, 733-9388). Opened in 1993, the Toronto Centre for the Arts (originally the Ford Centre for the Performing Arts) actually holds three theatres and the Museum of Contemporary Canadian Art.

A sterling feature of the Centre is the superb George Weston Recital Hall, described as a perfect setting for classical music. Curtains and panels can be manipulated to provide the most favourable acoustic balance, whatever the requirements. Solo recitals, chamber and small symphonic ensembles and dance recitals keep the hall busy all year. There are 1,000 seats on a main floor level. The Toronto Philharmonia Orchestra is the orchestra in residence. Average ticket prices range from $50 to $95.

Leave no trace — make sure your litter gets disposed of properly. Recycling containers are usually blue or silver.

THE VERTICALS

GIBSON HOUSE MUSEUM (5172 Yonge, 395-7432). Farther up Yonge just a stone's throw from the North York Civic Centre (see next page) stands Gibson House.

David Gibson came to Toronto in 1826. He married Eliza Milne and purchased the land for Gibson House. Like most of his neighbours, Gibson participated in the ill-fated Upper Canada Rebellion of 1837. He fled just ahead of Loyalist troops arriving to burn his house to the ground.

Pardoned by Queen Victoria in 1843, Gibson returned to his Yonge Street farm in 1851. There he and Eliza organized construction of a new home for their seven children. The red brick Georgian style home became a community focal point.

These days, the Museum brings history back to life with costumed guides, special events, and educational workshops (see Photo section). There's a continuous landscape on the entire north side of Park Home featuring a rose garden that merges the Gibson House garden with its surveyor-themed elements, alleviating the oppressive presence of nearby towering office buildings. Adults $2.75, seniors/students $2.25, children $1.75.

NORTH YORK CIVIC CENTRE — MEL LASTMAN SQUARE (5100 Yonge, 395-7350). This City of Toronto public square schedules concerts and events throughout the summer, with a special focus on cultural diversity. There is also a Farmers' Market every Thursday from 10 to 2 during the summer.

Before the amalgamation of Toronto, buildings around the square were City of North York Municipal Offices. Mel Lastman Square is named for the first and only Mayor of North York, who subsequently became Mayor of Toronto.

Shop at the local farmers' markets — be sure to bring your own shopping bag.

Things to Do, See, Buy & Eat

NORTH YORK CENTENNIAL SKATE SHOP (580 Finch W., inside Arena, 905-663-5841, www.centennialproshop.com) Buy and sell skate shop and sharpening. Specializes in goal tender equipment.

HISTORIC ZION SCHOOLHOUSE (1091 Finch E). Although you can't go in, take a walk past and enjoy this Gothic Revival building with a distinctive Georgian-like symmetry. It's located on the highest natural elevation site in Toronto.

DEMPSEY STORE (250 Beecroft). A local landmark, Dempsey store is one of the earliest surviving commercial properties in the area. It was relocated and designated for use as a facility for autistic children. Originally located at Yonge and Sheppard, it is now west of the **Gibson House Museum** (See page 140.)

YORK CEMETERY (101 Senlac Rd., 221-3404). This beautifully designed mid-twentieth century burial ground combines the strength of history with the eloquence of art. In front of the office, visit the bronze seagull sculpted by Sing Hoo Yuen, an internationally renowned artist and friend of the Group of Seven. Scattered throughout the grounds are four unique sundials, and an antique farm bell forms a central feature for a cremation garden.

Experience Toronto's cultural richness by taking part in local festivals and neighbourhood activities.

GEMS OF THE REGION

The items in this section may not link physically with the other areas in the guide, but these very special places are an integral part of the city's cultural, historical, artistic, scientific and recreational richness. Some are quite a trek from the streets and neighbourhoods already covered and some are just outside the city boundaries.

We start in the central west part of Toronto at Corso Italia, wind farther west through Etobicoke and then we make an arc over the city, coming back towards the lake in the east end of town. Just a little off the beaten track, you'll be treated to a lively neighbourhood, some incredible parks and absorbing gardens. You'll have the opportunity to learn about and visit an internationally renowned Canadian art collection, a globally respected observatory and a world famous zoo. So read on . . .

Highlights

DAVENPORT–PERTH COMMUNITY GARDEN
(1990 Davenport, behind Davenport-Perth Community Centre, 392-1668). This beautiful woodland garden provides an escape from the hustle and bustle of the city surrounding it.

STOP 103 COMMUNITY GARDEN (Earlscourt Park between St. Clair W. and Davenport, 392-1668). This garden supplies the foodbank at STOP 103, an important neighbourhood centre.

CORSO ITALIA (East and west from Dufferin along St. Clair W). Savour the sights, sounds, aromas, and feel of Italy all concentrated within a few blocks. Shops filled with European-styled high-fashion merchandise and restaurants specializing in a variety of regional cuisine can keep an active shopper busy and well-fed.

Corso Italia is Toronto's other Italian neighbourhood. Little Italy, in the College area, was the original neighbourhood of choice for emigrating Italian families in the 1920s. By the 1960s, Corso Italia was growing as many established Italian families chose to make the move north to escape the busy inner-city feel of the core. Italian lamp posts and potted plants lend a European flavour to the new heart of Toronto's Italian community. A bronze statue dedicated to Italian Canadian immigrant families is located on the south side of St. Clair beside the TTC loop at Lansdowne Avenue.

Why not try La Paloma Gelateria & Bar located at

1357 St. Clair 656-2340. It's one of Toronto's first authentic gelaterias.

PROSPECT CEMETERY, CREMATORIUM & MAUSOLEUM (1450 St. Clair W., 651-4040). This is a cemetery that is vibrant with life. Grounds brim with plants and animals. People of stone and marble seem ready to step from their pedestals. Tranquillity is so thorough, you can hear nature breathe. There is beauty, history and peace. Since the close of the 19th century, **Prospect Cemetery** — once a family farm — has remained both the embodiment and the antithesis of death. The celebration of art is a vital attribute of **Prospect Cemetery**. In the mausoleum, Contemporary Canadian artist Sarah Hall has created 14 stained glass windows representing the Stations of the Cross (see photo section). Constructed around bronze relief works by Joseph Stanek, these contemplative works illustrating the passionate observance of life's end emphasize not loss through death, but meaning through life. Symphonic mergers of colour and light soothe and gratify the senses, and are worth a visit.

You can read about gardeners' interests, events and other green thumb information in the Toronto Community Garden Network newsletter posted on www.foodshare.net/grow.htm.

ETOBICOKE WATERSHED. Etobicoke is at Toronto's western extreme. Comprised of the one-time farm area of Alderwood, the lakefront cottage communities of Long Branch and Mimico, and the industrial New Toronto, it is best defined through its relationship to the watersheds of Mimico and Etobicoke Creeks and the Humber River.

Long neglected in favour of development and industry, only in recent years has the environment become a focus for the community. This spirit is infectious. Etobicoke now benefits from local environmental activism. The results can be seen in any of the recovering parklands. Refer to the South Etobicoke Regeneration Project (see page 115).

Like most of early Toronto, settlement here was based on grants from the Crown. When the earliest Torontonians looked for more room, they began the spread toward Mimico and Etobicoke Creeks. Possessing the pioneer staples of fresh water to drink, adequate game and fertile land, the area drew homesteaders. Land grants were subdivided and lots were sold enabling settlers to gain a foothold.

Also worth visiting are the **Etobicoke Civic Centre Farmers Market** (Civic Centre parking lot, 399 The West Mall. 394-8526. Saturday 8 to 2, May to October) and **Etobicoke Civic Centre Art Gallery** (399 The West Mall, 394-8390).

MONTGOMERY'S INN (4709 Dundas W., 394-8113). One of the oldest buildings in Etobicoke, now restored as a living museum of the 1847-50 period, was built in about 1830 as a home for Thomas and Margaret Montgomery. Surrounded by a large farm, they operated the building as a hotel until 1859. Tenants farmed the land until the 1940s and the house / hotel is now open as a museum with a special focus on early Etobicoke artifacts. Year-round events invite participation from visitors. The Inn's costumed historical interpreters create the feeling of being at an inn long ago. Afternoon tea is served from 2-4, Tuesday to Sunday. Adults $3, seniors/students $2, children $1.

Montgomery's Inn

CENTENNIAL PARK & CONSERVATORY

(56 Centennial Park Rd., 394-8754). Be sure to go to one of the three greenhouses in this park. The fantastic conservatory has 1080 square metres (12,000 square feet) of plant collections. The park has nine picnic areas. (Permits are required for large gatherings). Facilities are available for hang gliding, para-gliding, Australian-rules football and disc golf. The park also has a 2,200-seat outdoor stadium.

HUMBER ARBORETUM (205 Humber College Blvd., 675-5009). An educational experience that both kids and adults can share and enjoy is a rare find. This carefully maintained arboretum just south of Finch along the West Humber River delivers that experience.

Learning is constant on the self-guided trails as you become completely absorbed in your surroundings.The centrepiece here is the Nature Orientation Centre with its assortment of ever-changing displays and exhibits.

A circular wooden deck offers visitors a bird's eye view of much of the Arboretum. From here, the Dunnington Grubb Gardens present themselves as the first stop along the way. A Woodlot and Meadow Garden of ash, maple, beech and ironwood trees borders a naturalized meadow with over 5,000 plants typical of the area. A trail leads to the Demonstration Gardens further east with its collection of native woody plants most suitable for the urban environment. This is a goldmine of planting, growing and design ideas for the home gardener.

McMICHAEL COLLECTION (10365 Islington, 905-893-1121). The McMichael Canadian Art Collection is in the village of Kleinburg, 30 kilometres (19 miles) north west of downtown Toronto. A main feature of the gallery is the work of The Group of Seven (which grew to include ten members, six of whom are buried in a small cemetery on the McMichael grounds: Arthur Lismer, Frederick Varley, Lawren Harris, Frank Johnston, A.J. Casson and A.Y. Jackson).

As well as many temporary installations throughout the year, the McMichael features a collection of contemporary First Nations art along with prints, drawings and sculpture by Inuit artists representing the Northwest Territories and northern Quebec. In addition, drawings, prints and sculpture representing the archival collection of the West Baffin Eskimo Co-operative in Cape Dorset are on long term loan.

Enjoy the rugged surrounding lands for hikes, picnics, and photography. The grounds are lovely and trails are wheelchair accessible. Adults $9, seniors/students/children $7, children under 5 free.

KORTRIGHT CENTRE FOR CONSERVATION AND CENTRE FOR SUSTAINABLE LIVING (9550 Pine Valley Dr., 661-6600 or 905-832-2289). In an almost pristine location on the Humber River, in Woodbridge (just north of Toronto) lies Canada's largest environmental installation.

It has162 hectares (400 acres) of forest, meadows, and Humber Valley wetlands. Rich in bird, plant, and animal life, its "back to nature" programs offer a year-round living, breathing, environmental classroom, including Canada's largest demonstration of renewable energy technology.

Over 18 kilometres (11 miles) of trails through mixed woods and open parkland ensure ample access to a full range of recreational and educational options (a special treat for spring visitors, freshly tapped maple syrup from the on-site sugar bush). (See Photo section.)

This centre offers programs and hands-on activities for all ages. Interesting options include native plant tours, energy displays of solar power and windmills and more. Regular admission: Adults $5 seniors / students / children $3.

The average person in Canada produces 2.2 kg of garbage per day. 30

BLACK CREEK PIONEER VILLAGE (1000 Murray Ross Pkwy., 736-1733). Visit **Black Creek Pioneer Village** and spiral back in time to the 19th century with more than 35 carefully restored 1860s Victorian village shops and homes (See Photo section). Costumed hosts guide you through Canadian history where you can talk to the blacksmith, the tinsmith, the cabinet maker and others about their crafts. Visit the doctor's house, Roblin's Mill and water wheel, and take home stone ground flour milled before your very eyes.

Pioneer gardens feature traditional herbs, vegetables, perennials and more. Enjoy a scrumptious lunch at the Halfway House. The Village offers free wagon rides and other activities to the kids. **Black Creek Pioneer Village** is open from May 1 to December 31 (closed Christmas Day) and hosts many special events throughout the year. Adults $9, seniors/students $7, children $5.

DOWNSVIEW DELLS (Sheppard W., midway between Jane and Keele south of Downsview Park, 392-1111). This great picnic location is found along a secluded, heavily forested section of the Black Creek valley. Open fields for casual sports, hiking and cross-country skiing and wooded areas ideal for nature walks and wildlife viewing are features of this park.

DOWNSVIEW PARK (PARC DOWNSVIEW PARK) (Sheppard W. between Keele and Allan Expwy., 952-2233). Here land that was once used by the

Department of National Defence is being transformed into a unique 130 hectare (322 acres) urban green space. The land originally farmed by the Boake family before being acquired by the Federal government will almost come full circle, reverting to a more natural state.

This is the highest point of table-land in the City of Toronto, and many small tributaries that feed the Humber and Don river systems issue from here. When the Canadian Forces Base Toronto (Downsview) was closed recently, its lands were dedicated to become "Canada's first national urban park". Lively public discourse continues to shape the vision for this site.

"Tree City" is the design concept featuring a variety of landscape elements that will be incorporated over time. The park will evolve in response to a balance of environmental, social and economic demands. In the first phase soil will be prepared to become self-restorative, a protective feature vital to the survival of the Park. Supplemented by meadowlands, water features, sports fields, and gardens, the Park will eventually become self-sustaining. In time, the Park will constitute a key link in Toronto's system of conservation areas and parks, creating a network of multi-use public lands.

Watch for annual events, year-round educational and cultural activities, and guided walking tours.

90% of Torontonians are very concerned about the environment. [31]

G. ROSS LORD PARK (Dufferin and Finch, 392-1111). North of Finch this park was established in 1972 mainly as a flood control dam that protects the communities of Hogg's Hollow. A series of naturalization projects began to enhance and replenish native trees, shrubs and wildflowers. Pine, oak, maple, aspen, and cherry trees have been planted and, when a sustainable forest canopy has formed, shade-tolerant species like Hazel and Serviceberry will further diversify the woodland portion of the park.

Active recreational options include cross-country skiing, cricket, and bird watching. This park is also the home of the Community Association for Horse Riding for the Disabled (667-8600).

DAVID DUNLAP OBSERVATORY (DDO) (123 Hillsview Dr., 905-884-2112). This is the site of the largest optical telescope in Canada and it carries out active public education and teaching programmes. Located in Richmond Hill, a community just north of Toronto, DDO is a research centre of the Department of Astronomy in the Faculty of Arts and Sciences at the University of Toronto. Tours are offered, although children under 7 are not permitted.

BETTY SUTHERLAND TRAIL (Duncan Mill Rd. to Sheppard). This trail leads through valley wilderness at the northern end of the West Don River in Toronto. A wild river valley sanctuary, it still has the original farmhouse of one-time owner George S. Henry, the former Ontario Premier who purchased the land in 1898.

Once the trail construction was completed, landscape naturalization featured the planting of native trees, shrubs and wildflowers that enhance and improve the area as a wildlife habitat.

EARL BALES PARK (Bathurst and Sheppard, 395-7922). A valley park with excellent picnic potential, the park also includes the 1500-seat Barry Zukerman Amphitheatre and Holocaust Memorial. You can also downhill ski and cross-country ski on groomed trails during the winter here, and catch site of mature black walnut, sugar maple, American beech and black maple trees. At the northern end of the park is the Hinder Property, a sheltered habitat for birds and other wildlife. Located near Highway 401, this park is a reclaimed golf course. In fact, the tees and greens are still identifiable as you walk about. The original Bales homestead built in 1824 actually remains intact at the north west corner.

TORONTO ZOO & BOTANICAL GARDENS (361A Old Finch, 392-5900). Overlooking the Rouge Valley, the Toronto Zoo provides a 287 hectare (710 acre) home to over 4,000 animals and birds from all over the world. Animals are grouped according to geographical origin in seven different pavilions. Hardier animals have large open exhibit areas in which to roam, so bring a camera. Young children thrill at their first sight of elephants and giraffes, while inquisitive visitors learn about the ecosystem of the Amazon.

Water-based exhibits include polar bears, south African fur seals, beavers/otters, and a South American waterfall.

The Indoor Zoo has pavilions for Africa, the Americas, IndoMalaya, Australasia, Indian Rhino, Guar and a Malayan Woods.

During the summer months the Zoomobile train takes passengers through the heart of the park past 40- metre cliffs and sugar maple forests. Wildlife settings are complemented by natural woodlands and created habitats. From the train you can see examples of wetlands and wildflower-butterfly meadows. Other creature comforts like washrooms, snack bars and picnic tables are conveniently located throughout the zoo. Visitors are welcome any time as the park is open all year round. Adults $13, seniors $10, children $8, children under 3 free.

And all the excitement isn't contained within the zoo. Salmon run in the nearby Rouge River and a bear was sighted nearby (his footprints were found under the 401 highway). Even a cougar has been spotted in this area — its wilderness unconstrained.

Rouge Park is the largest North American natural and cultural heritage park in an urban area. When complete, parklands will protect over 4640 hectares (11,600 acres) of valley and tablelands from Lake Ontario to the Oak Ridges Moraine. 32

ROUGE PARK (East end of Toronto along the Rouge River, 392-8186 or 905-713-6007).The Rouge River and its tributaries from Lake Ontario to the Oak Ridges Moraine are home to an amazing diversity of wildlife and plants, including rare Carolinian species. The Rouge Marsh is the best remaining example of a lakeshore marsh in Toronto. When completed, the Park will be 4,700 hectares (11750 acres) in size.

One of the best ways to explore the **Rouge Park** is to hike along designated trails (although signage can be sparse). Don't forget your binoculars — a white-tailed deer, a scarlet tanager or a Cooper's hawk may be just around the next corner.

The **Rouge Park** Vision is to be a special place of outstanding natural features and diverse cultural heritage in an urban-rural setting that is protected and flourishing as an ecosystem well into the future. **Rouge Park** naturalists aim to help human activities exist in harmony with the natural elements of the park and provide a sanctuary for nature and the human spirit. To get involved in tree planting and other initiatives, contact Save the Rouge Valley System. (See Resource Groups page 151.)

GUILD INN / GUILDWOOD PARK (201 Guildwood Pkwy., 261-3331). Mammoth keystones, fanciful doorways and stone archways to nowhere await you here, mementoes salvaged from the demolition of some of Toronto's historic buildings. (See Photo section.) Opened in the 1930s as a rent-free artist's colony, the inn today offers a fine-dining restaurant and hotel accommodation (phone ahead). Cresting Scarborough Bluffs, the cultivated gardens and park verges are rich in wildlife and flowers. Trilliums and trout lilies bloom in the naturalized forest. Behind the inn is a 19th century log cabin similar to the homes built by Toronto's first settlers. The cabin and its site are part of an ongoing archaeological excavation and are open to the public free of charge in the summer.

CEDAR RIDGE STUDIO GALLERY (225 Confederation Dr., 396-4112 or 396-4026). This arts centre is located in charming historic buildings surrounded by formal gardens and parkland. It combines gallery space and working studios. Educational, recreational and cultural programs as well as juried competitions are features at Cedar Ridge.

Bird watching in Toronto? Yes! Peregrine falcons on Bay St., cormorants in Tommy Thompson Park, hawks in High Park . . . Toronto is along one of the major migratory routes for many species of birds. Call the Toronto Field Naturalists (593-2656) for info on bird watching tours held in and around the city. 33

HIGHLAND CREEK (Kingston Rd. and Highland Creek Dr., 392-8186). The Highland Creek Restoration project, which began in 1998, has done much to restore this area to its original condition. Over 1100 trees and shrubs have been planted by various groups, including Friends of the Highland (439-1036). Community and school plantings have helped, and a snake hibernaculum has also been constructed.

It's a big city, but you can easily get out for the day to see a play at Stratford Festival (1-800-567-1600) or Shaw Festival(1-800-511-7429) or visit Richter's Herb farm (905-640-6677). Or take a hike through beautiful woodlands along the Bruce Trail (www.brucetrail.org). Many areas surrounding Toronto are accessible by public transit or commuter rail. Visit www.city.toronto.on.ca/ttc or www.gotransit.com for destinations and schedules.

THOMPSON MEMORIAL PARK AND SCARBOROUGH HISTORICAL MUSEUM (1007 Brimley Rd., 431-3441). Historical landmarks at Thompson

Memorial Park include the "Springfield House," built in 1840, and St. Andrew's Presbyterian Church, built in 1849 on land donated by David Thompson. The museum in Thompson Memorial Park plays a vital role by preserving and presenting Toronto's rich heritage dating from 1796. Tours are offered. Adults $2,seniors/children $1.

Resource Groups

Toronto is an active community. There are resource groups and organizations involved in so many important things. You may be inspired to spend some of your time here in the community planting a tree, cleaning up a river, or learning about cultural history. We couldn't possibly tell you about everything happening in Toronto, but we do offer some useful resources to start you off.

Environmental / Community

ADVOCACY FOR RESPECT FOR CYCLISTS
(504-2918, x1, www.web.net/~detour/arc). Information and support for Toronto cyclists.

ACTION TO RESTORE A CLEAN HUMBER (ARCH)
(21 Taysham Cres., 741-5346). Activities range from stream/wetland monitoring, to restoration and pollution prevention for the Humber River. Also does tree planting events along the Humber.

AUTOSHARE (24 Mercer, 340-7888, www.autoshare.com). Car sharing, a more sustainable alternative to owning a car.

BLOOR WEST ECO-VILLAGE (769-4344). Runs workshops on environmental topics and raises environmental issues with all levels of government, participates in volunteer community clean-ups, and takes part in local environmental events.

COMMUNITY BICYCLE NETWORK (CBN) (761 Queen W., 504-2918). Co-ordinates and helps recycle donated bikes for distribution to various community groups working with the underprivileged in Toronto.

CITIZENS ENVIRONMENT WATCH (CEW) (978-4144, www.utoronto.ca/envstudy/cew/cew/html). Promotes local involvement with environmental monitoring.

CITIZENS CONCERNED ABOUT THE FUTURE OF THE ETOBICOKE WATERSHED (CCFEW) (661-6600, x 5334). Citizens group which acts and educates on the Etobicoke watershed.

DETOUR PUBLICATIONS (www.detourpublications. com). A one-stop on-line shop for books, magazines and other resources on sustainable transportation.

EVERGREEN (596-1495, www.evergreen.ca). Works to create a living city through education, tree planting and other events.

FRIENDS OF THE DON EAST (410-7153). Committed to the pursuit of local and regional actions to preserve and protect remaining natural areas within the city.

GREEN$AVER (203-3106, www.greensaver.org). Has conducted over 7,000 audits that save money and energy in the home.

GREENEST CITY (922-7626, www.greenestcity.org). Promotes sustainability and green practices and is committed to reducing pollution, regenerating urban life and promoting social equity.

HARBOURFRONT PARK SYSTEM (392-8186). This Toronto Parks and Recreation infoline provides information on picnic permits, the harbour ferry boat service and the Toronto islands.

KNIVES AND FORKS ADVOCATES FOR ORGANIC AGRICULTURE (422-1944). Promotes organic agriculture and environmental conscientiousness.

MOVING THE ECONOMY (www.city.toronto.on.ca/mte). Promotes and develops economic opportunities and innovations in sustainable transportation.

ONTARIO STREAMS (www.ontariostreams.on.ca). Actively rehabilitates wetlands and streams in the Toronto region.

ONTARIO CYCLING ASSOCIATION (www.ontario cycling.org). Info on cycling tours and clubs throughout the province.

PEOPLE & PLANET FRIENDLY EVENTS AND RESOURCES (www.planetfriendly.net.) This email newsletter lists current issues and events regarding sustainability and environmental responsibility.

RECYCLING COUNCIL OF ONTARIO (960-1025, www.rco.on.ca). Recycling information and education.

ROOFTOP GARDENS RESOURCE GROUP (www.interlog.com/~rooftop/). Promotes rooftop gardens and related groups/events in Toronto.

SAVE THE ROUGE VALLEY SYSTEM (282-9983). Volunteer members work to preserve and enhance the natural environment in the Rouge Valley. They also organize clean up days and tree planting — call ahead.

TASK FORCE TO BRING BACK THE DON (392-0401). Works towards "bringing back" a clean, green, and accessible Don River Watershed. They have spearheaded the planning of more than 35,000 trees and shrubs and thousands of wildflowers.

TORONTO COMMUNITY GARDEN NETWORK (392-1668, www.foodshare.net/grow.htm). Encourages a healthy community gardening movement in Toronto.

TORONTO ENVIRONMENTAL ALLIANCE (TEA) (596-0660, www.torontoenvironment.org). Provides opportunities for Toronto citizens to work together to develop local solutions to environmental problems. They have produced a useful *Use It Re-Use It* guide.

TORONTO & REGION CONSERVATION AUTHORITY (TRCA) (661-6600, www.trca.on.ca). Information on over 4,000 hectares (10,000 acres) of green space in Toronto.

TORONTO FIELD NATURALIST'S CLUB (593-2656). Excellent resource for information and other wildlife habitats.

TORONTO VEGETARIAN ASSOCIATION (544-9800, www.veg.on.ca). Provides info on vegetarian restaurants, organic markets and other resources.

TORONTO RENEWABLE ENERGY CO-OPERATIVE (TREC) (977-5093. www.trec.on.ca). Canada's first green energy co-operative with a mission is to promote renewable energy through education, advocacy, and project development.

WATERFRONT REGENERATION TRUST (943-8080, www.waterfronttrust.com). Promotes the protection and restoration of Toronto's waterfront.

WILDLANDS LEAGUE (971-9453, www.wildleague.org). Conservation group that works for Ontario's Wilderness.

Arts / Heritage / Culture / Social Justice

THE CENTRE FOR SOCIAL JUSTICE (www.socialjustice.com). Builds partnerships with various social movements to promote equality, and economic and social justice.

HERITAGE TORONTO (MUSEUMS AND HERITAGE SERVICES, CITY OF TORONTO) (205 Yonge, 392-6827, www.torontohistory.on.ca). Operates museums for the City of Toronto and promotes heritage preservation.

HERITAGE YORK (4066 Old Dundas, 767-5472). Works to preserve the historical heritage of the City of York through education programs that increase awareness

HIGH PARK CITIZENS ADVISORY COMMITTEE (392-1748, x 5 for tours). Well-established year-round group showcases the natural and cultural history of High Park.

MULTICULTURAL HISTORY SOCIETY OF ONTARIO (979-2973). Dedicated to telling the stories of Canada's people, fosters understanding and social cohesion and showcases the benefits of our diversity.

NATIVE CANADIAN CENTRE (964-9087). Various social, recreational and cultural programs with a focus on Native culture.

TORONTO HISTORICAL ASSOCIATION (425-4643). An umbrella organization that represents over 60 museums, heritage sites and organizations involved in Toronto's natural and cultural heritage.

Tourism / Other

ATTRACTIONS ONTARIO (868-4386, www.attractions. on.ca). Promotes Ontario tourism and attractions.

ECOTOURISM SOCIETY (www.ecotourism.org). Tips and lessons about ecotourism and choosing eco-operators.

TRAVEL BY RAIL AND MUCH MORE (701-0756, www.travelbyrail.com). Tourism consulting and information on rail holidays.

Member Listings

The following businesses and organizations, highlighted in green type throughout this guide, have pledged to an ongoing vision of urban green tourism.

They have signed on as members to actively support and share the Green Tourism Association's mission both in practice and in principle with respect to fostering ecological responsibility, local economic vitality, cultural sensitivity, and experiential richness through tourism.

Our mission: ***To develop and cultivate a green tourism industry within the Toronto region; an industry which is ecologically sound, fosters appreciation of and respect for diverse cultural and natural heritage, and strengthens local economies and communities.***

The community of green tourism trailblazers grows every day. Please check our website for new members' listings at www.greentourism.on.ca.

Category Icons

To make this guide easier to use we're using the same Green Map System™ icons that found in "The Other Map."

- Green Space & Parklands
- Naturalization Sites
- Special Gardens
- General or Sustainable Transportation
- Bike Sites
- Museums & Heritage Sites
- Art Galleries
- Shopping
- Restaurants & Cafés
- Organic Produce & Natural Foods
- Tours
- Accommodations
- Resource Group
- Environmental Visits
- Festivals and Events
- Visitor Information

Special Designation Icons

We also highlight special features for each listing.

- Smoke Free
- Educational Programs offered
- Environmental literature displayed
- Tours offered
- Bike parking available
- Recycling containers available
- Wheelchair Access

Member Index by Category

Accommodation

Bed & Breakfast Association of Downtown Toronto
Delta Chelsea Hotel
Fairmont Hotels & Resorts
Hostelling International
Indian Line Campground
Les Amis Vegetarian Bed and Breakfast
Marigold International Travellers Hostel
Mimico Hostel and Bed & Breakfast
Neill-Wycik College Hostel
Ryerson Polytechnic University Conference Services
Sutton Place Hotel

Transportation

AutoShare
Bathurst Cycle
Cycle Path - Danforth
Cycle Path - Yonge
McBride Cycle and Sports
Moving the Economy
Recycle Bike Company (Set Me Free) - Queen Street
Recycle Bike Company (Set Me Free) - Roncesvalles
StreetCity Bikes
Travel by Rail and Much More
Wheel Excitement

Food

Natural Foods:
- ACE Bakery
- Advantage Health Matters
- Baldwin Natural Foods
- Big Carrot Natural Food Market

Karma Food Co-op
Sephiroth
Restaurants/Cafés/Microbreweries:
Alternative Grounds Coffeehouse & Roastery
Bacchus Roti Shop
Health Haven
Le Commensal Fine Vegetarian Cuisine
Steam Whistle Brewery

Green Stores

Birders Nature Store - Bloor West
Birders Nature Store - Eglinton
Ecoworks
Eternal Moment Bookstore
Grassroots Environmental Products - Bloor West
Grassroots Environmental Products - Danforth
Gwendolyne Hats
Kluane's Creations
Mountain Equipment Co-op

Tours

A Stroll in the Park Walking and Adventure Club
A Taste of the World
More Than Just Walking
ROM Walks
Skyland Tours Ltd.

Green Spaces

Albion Hills Conservation Area
Boyd Conservation Area
Bruce's Mill Conservation Area
Glen Haffy Conservation Area
Heart Lake Conservation Area
Mount Pleasant Cemetery
Petticoat Creek Conservation Area
Pine Hills Cemetery
Prospect Cemetery
Rouge Park
Tommy Thompson Park
Toronto Necropolis
York Cemetery

Museum/Heritage Sites

Black Creek Pioneer Village
Campbell House
Colborne Lodge
Fort York
Gibson House Museum
The Lambton House (Heritage York)
Mackenzie House

Montgomery's Inn
Museum for Textiles
Scarborough Historical Museum
Spadina House and Gardens
The Pier: Toronto's Waterfront Museum
Todmorden Mills Museum (City of Toronto)

Festivals & Events

Festive Earth Society
Great White North Communications Inc.

Environmental Visits

Harbourfront Centre
Humber Arboretum
Kortright Centre for Conservation
Ontario Science Centre

Art Galleries

Armen Art Gallery
Broken Fence Society
Carrier Gallery
Cedar Ridge Studio Gallery & Botanical Gardens
Found Objects Internet Cafe & Gallery
Market Gallery

Resource Groups

Danforth by the Valley BIA
Detour Publications
Evergreen
Friends of the Don East
Greenest City
Green$aver
Hotel Employees, Restaurant Employees Union, Local 75
Humber College- HRT Alliance
International Ecotourism Society
People & Planet Friendly Events and Resources
Riverdale Community Business Centre
Sir Sandford Fleming College
Toronto & Region Conservation Authority
Toronto Cycling Committee
Toronto Historical Association
Tourism Environment
Tourism Toronto
West Toronto Junction Historical Society
401 Richmond Limited

Individuals

Agboola Abiodun
Anita Kmecz
Lele Truong

Alphabetical Member Listings

A Stroll in the Park Walking and Adventure Club

484-WALK (9255). 10th year in 2000! Fun group walks for singles on weekends in Toronto's beautiful parks! Fun special trips. New members get 3 free walks. Couples and Toronto visitors welcome! 99% single. www.interlog.com/~walktalk/

A Taste of the World - Neighbourhood Bicycle Tours and Walks Inc.

923-6813. Offering off-the-beaten path theme tours since 1993. Experience a neighbourhood with new eyes and palates. Walks include Haunted Kensington, Old and New Chinatowns, Bike: More Than An Island, and more. Each tour starts at a different place. 8:30am–9:30pm year-round. www.torontowalksbikes.com

ACE Bakery

1 Hafis Rd. 241-3600. European-influenced, hand-shaped bread, made with the finest all-natural ingredients and free of additives or preservatives. Ten percent of net pre-tax profits go to Calmeadow, a Canadian non-profit organization that provides small loans to home-based enterprises. There is also a café. Lawrence W.@ Keele. M–Sat: 10–4. www.ace-bakery.com

Advantage Health Matters

4884 Dufferin, Unit 4. 667-7077. Importer and distributor of high-quality health food products. Non–genetically modified and certified organic. Steeles@ Dufferin M–Sat: 9–5. www.synergy-co.com

Albion Hills Conservation Area and Campground

16500 Highway 50. 667-6299 or 1-800-838-9921. The oldest conservation area in Ontario. You can picnic, swim, camp, canoe, fish, bike, hike, ski, toboggan, birdwatch and more in and along Albion Hills exciting trails, streams,

MEMBER LISTINGS

forests, and wetlands. Highway 50 @ Highway 9, 8km N of Bolton. 9–dusk (seasonal). www.trca.on.ca/vtab0.html

Alternative Grounds Coffee House & Roastery

333 Roncesvalles Ave. 534-5543. A community-based café and roastery specializing in freshly-roasted and fairly-traded coffees, including a number of organic and decaffeinated varieties. We also offer fairly-traded tea. Roncesvalles @ Howard Park. Sun–Th 8–8, F–Sat 8am–9:30pm.

Armen Art Gallery

A

16 Wellesley W. 924-5375. A wide selection of Canadian First Nation arts and crafts, originals, soapstone carvings, pottery and jewellery. Yonge @ Wellesley M–F 10–6, Sat 11–6.

Auto Share

T

340-7888. Car sharing network for Torontonians. The smart alternative to owning a car provides all the mobility you need without the hassles, expense and pollution of owning a car. Pick up cars along the subway routes and at various locations across Toronto. Pay by the hour. Reservations: 24 hours. www.autoshare.com

Bacchus Roti Shop

1376 Queen W. 532-8191. West Indian restaurant established in 1985, serving roties, rice and a variety of curry meats and vegetables. M–W: 11–10, Th–Sat: 11–11.

Bathurst Cycle

913 Bathurst 533-7510. Brand name bicycle parts and accessories at reasonable cost. Bicycle repairs done quickly and efficiently. Also trades used bikes and rents bicycles. Summer 8–8, Winter 10–6.

Baldwin Naturals

20 Baldwin 979-1777. Specializes in organic produce, organic and natural groceries, meats, and dairy; supplements, herbal remedies, bulk herbs, skincare and aromatherapy. Organic deli and juice bar. University @ Dundas. M–W 10–7, Th–F 10–9, Sat 9:30–6, Sun 11–5.

Bed & Breakfast Association of Downtown Toronto

410-3938. Representing Toronto's largest selection of fully inspected B & B homes all centrally located within 10 minutes of major attractions. Parking available. 9–6. www.bnbinfo.com

The Big Carrot

348 Danforth Ave. 466-2129. Toronto's largest natural food worker/owner co-operative, specializing in products that are minimally processed, organically grown, cruelty-free and environmentally safe. Also offers an expanded bodycare department and a holistic dispensary. (Thursday nights: tours & free seminars - phone to book). Danforth @ Chester Ave. M–W 9:30–7, Th–F 9:30–9, Sat 9:30–6, Sun 11–5. www.thebigcarrot.ca

Birders Nature Store (Bloor)

2100 Bloor W. 604-9272. An ever-changing array of the fancy, the frivolous and the functional for the back yard naturalist. Bloor @ Keele. 9–7.

Birders Nature Store (Eglinton Ave).

265 Eglinton Ave. W 481-2431. Wild bird feeding specialists. Bird houses and feeders and bat houses. Nature books and bird guides. Yard and garden décor and nature giftware. Eglinton @ Oriole Parkway. M–F 10–7, Sat 10–6, Sun 12–5.

Black Creek Pioneer Village

1000 Murray Ross Pkwy. 736-1733. A brilliantly recreated 1860s country village where the people, crafts, trades and architecture of a colourful by-gone era bring Canada's past alive again. Jane @ Steeles. 7 days a week from May 1–Dec 31. www.trca.on.ca/bcpv.html

Boyd Conservation Area

8739 Islington Ave. 667-6299. With lush green grasses, forests and nature trails, it's hard to believe that this area is right in the middle of increasing urban development. Renowned as a première picnic location, Boyd also offers tranquillity, great bird and wildlife watching, and much more. Islington @ Rutherford. 5km N of Highway 7. 9–dusk (spring–fall). www.trca.on.ca/4ab.html

The Broken Fence Society

A

68 Broadview Ave., Suite 413. 469-0153. A visual arts collective educating children and adults about environmental issues through art shows, newsletters, calendars and other art events presented in various venues throughout the city. Broadview @ Queen E. M&F 10–5, S&S 10–4.

Bruce's Mill Conservation Area

3291 Stouffville Rd. 667-6299. This beautiful setting is home to the Mill Pond, a popular bacteria-free swimming hole; the Sugarbush Maple Syrup Festival; incredible fall colours and serene winter hiking, cross-country skiing or snowshoeing. Stouffville @ Warden 3 km E of Highway 404. 9–dusk (seasonal). www.trca.on.ca/4ac.html

Campbell House

Ⓣ

160 Queen W. 597-0227. The oldest remaining building from the Town of York has been beautifully restored to provide visitors with a glimpse of Toronto in the 1820s through tours, programs and special events by costumed

guides. Queen @ University Summer: M–F 9:30–4:30, wkds & holidays 12–4:30. Winter: M–F 9:30–4:30. www.advsoc.on.ca/campbell/GoCampbellHouse

Carrier Gallery

Columbus Centre - 901 Lawrence Ave. W. 789-7011 x 245. The Joseph D. Carrier Gallery promotes established and emerging Canadian artists and those of Italian heritage. It is also dedicated to presenting culturally specific exhibitions from around the world. Parkland and picnic tables available as part of the community centre. Lawrence W @ Dufferin. M–F: 12–5, Sat: 12–4.

Cedar Ridge Creative Centre

225 Confederation Dr. 396-4026. A centre for the arts located in charming historic buildings surrounded by formal gardens and parkland, combining gallery space and working studios. Offers educational, recreational and cultural opportunities. Presents juried contemporary and regular gallery programming. Facility rentals available. Scarborough Golf Club @ Lawrence E., S. 9–5, some nights open late, Summer 9–5. http://crsg.findhere.com

Colborne Lodge

1 Colborne Lodge Dr. (in High Park). 392-6916. This museum was the 19th Century home of John and Jemima Howard, founders of High Park. Lakeshore @ Parkside. May–Dec: Tu–Sun afternoons, Jan–April: wkd afternoons. www.city.toronto.on.ca/culture

The Cyclepath (Danforth)

1510 Danforth Ave. 463-5346. From a beginner mountain bike to a 23-pound race-ready trail ripper. From a single-gear cruiser (yes, just like you used to ride in the '50s, grandpa!) to a bike path and street-friendly hybrid. From Junior's first, (Thanks MOM& DAD) to Junior's last! Bike and in-line skate sales and service, repairs and all accessories. Danforth @ Coxwell. Summer: M–W 10–8, Th–F 10–9, Sat 10–6, Sun

12–5. Winter: M–F 10–7, Sat 10–6. www.thecyclepath.com

The Cyclepath (Yonge)

2106 Yonge 487-1717. Quality, name brand bicycles and accessories to suit any kind of riding, and any kind of budget. Experts in retail and service of bicycles, related accessories and fitness equipment. Rentals available. Yonge @ Davisville. M–F 10–9, Sat 10–6, Sun 12–5. www.thecyclepath.com

Danforth by the Valley Business Improvement Area

140 Danforth Ave. 429-4479. Representing hundreds of businesses in the Danforth area. A scenic district with multicultural cuisine and fabulous shopping. Please call for information. Special events: Taste of the Danforth, 2nd week of August every year, in association with Greek Town BIA. Danforth @ Broadview

Delta Chelsea Hotel

33 Gerrard W. 595-1975. A four-diamond property, the Delta Chelsea is Canada's largest hotel with 1591 guest rooms, two restaurants and three lounges. Located in the heart of downtown Toronto. They have an environmental program. Yonge @ Gerrard. www.deltachelsea.com

Detour Publications

500 University Ave., 8th Fl. 338-5087 (call ahead). Detour Publications is a one-stop source for a broad and growing range of books, videos, and reference materials on sustainable transportation and urban ecology. Titles are sold online, by mail order or in person.University @ Dundas. www.detourpublications.com

The International Ecotourism Society

An international non-profit organization dedicated to creating sustainable ecotravel experiences, seeks to inform travellers about how their "Travel Choice Makes a

Difference." For a free consumer guide, contact P.O. Box 668, Burlington, VT 05402, U.S.A. 802-447-2121. www.ecotourism.org/travelchoice

Ecoworks

An innovative planet-friendly gift service. Customers can create personalized gift boxes from a selection of environmentally-friendly products such as fair trade coffee, original pottery, handmade soaps, and tree-free journals. M–F 10–6, S&S 10–5. Call first.

The Eternal Moment Bookstore

924-3780. Bookstore and boutique focusing on personal development with a touch of the mystic. Bloor @ Bathurst. M–Sat 10–9, Sun 10–7. www.interlog.com/~eternal

Evergreen

355 Adelaide W., 5th Fl. 596-1495, toll free 1-888-426-3138. Evergreen can help you restore the natural health of Toronto - at school, in the community and at home by supplying resources, providing training and leading site restoration activities. Spadina subway - take streetcar S to Adelaide M–F 9–5. www.evergreen.ca

Fairmont Hotels & Resorts

Fairmont Hotels & Resorts is the largest luxury hotel management company in North America. Since 1990, its award-winning Green Partnership program has remained the industry leader for environmental stewardship.

For more information on Fairmont's environmental affairs and procedures call 874-2600.

The Royal York is one of the industry leaders in environmentally-friendly initiatives. It's green from the top of its roof, where the chef grows his herb garden, down to the very sub-basement, where workers sort through all bins in the recycling depot. Reservations phone 1-800-663-7229. 100 Front Union subway or via the underground PATH system. www.fairmont.com

Festive Earth Society

469-2977. FES produces seasonal celebrations, educational programs, and forums to build networks of green partnerships for local environmental and economic development. M–F 9–5. www.festiveearth.com

Fort York

100 Garrison Rd. 392-6907. Fort York is home to Canada's largest collection of original War of 1812 buildings. It is also a national historical site. Lakeshore @ Strachan. Summer: M–Sun 10–5. Winter: M–F 10–4, S&S 10–5.

Found Object: Internet Café and Post-Consumption Gift Shop

657 College 588-9600. Also sells environmental art. College subway. Bathurst @ College. Summer: 12–8. Winter: 10–8. www.foundobject.net

Friends of the Don East (FODE)

For information about tree planting efforts and events, call 381-0240. FODE is committed to the pursuit of local and regional actions that will preserve, protect and enhance the remaining natural areas within our city.

Gibson House Museum

5172 Yonge 395-7432. Visitors to this beautiful Georgian farmhouse explore the lives of the Gibson family in the rural community of Willowdale in 1851. Yonge @ Park Home. Tu–F 9:30–4:30, wkds & hols 12–5. www.city.toronto.on.ca\culture

Glen Haffy Conservation Area

(no wheelchair bathrooms)

19305 Airport Rd. 667-6299. Where the Oak Ridges Moraine meets the Niagara Escarpment, Glen Haffy offers you dramatic hills, mature forests, great fall colours, scenic hiking and biking trails, and breathtaking views. Glen Haffy has stocked trout ponds and hosts fishing derbies in spring/summer, and Pumpkinfest in fall. Airport Rd. @ Highway 9. 9–dusk (spring–fall).www.trca.on.ca/4ae.html

Grassroots Environmental Products (Bloor)

Ⓣ

408 Bloor W. 944-1993. Grassroots is your one-stop environmental shop, providing you with the choices you need to live a healthy earth-friendly life. Non-toxic, biodegradable personal and cleaning products, air and water filtration, hemp articles and gardening alternatives. Bloor @ Brunswick. M–F 10–8, Sat 10–6, Sun 12–6. www.grassrootsstore.com

Grassroots Environmental Products (Danforth)

Ⓣ

372 Danforth Ave. 466-2841. Chester subway. M–Th 10–7, F 10–8, Sat 10–6, Sun 12–6. www.grassrootsstore.com

Great White North Communications Inc.

25 Polson 2nd Fl. 962-8899. This event marketing company specialises in the sport of dragon boat racing. Bay subway - N to Davenport.Summer: 9–9. Winter: 9–6. www.dragon-boat.com

Greenest City

922-7626. A non-profit, community-based environmental organization committed to reducing pollution, regenerating urban life and promoting social equity. 9:30–5:30. www.greenestcity.org

Green$aver

51 Wolseley, 5th Fl. 203-3106. A non-profit organization that tests your home's energy efficiency and solves your home's heating and comfort problems with a team of retrofit experts. Bathurst @ Queen. M–F 9–7. www.greensaver.org

Gwendolyne Hats

401 Richmond W, Suite 433. 351-1219. Modern classics assembled by hand with love and care. Sent out into the world to foster individuality, joy and spirit. One-of-a-kind hats for women and men are designed, created and sold on the premises. Our palette is a rich combination of diverse colours, luxurious textures and ornate patterns. Richmond @ Queen W. Tu–F 12–6, Sat 12–5.www.gwendolynehats.com

Harbourfront Centre

York Quay Centre, 235 Queen's Quay W. 973-3000. Canada's foremost centre for contemporary culture, including performing arts, festivals, reading series, visual arts exhibitions, craft studios, family programmes, and more. Queen's Quay W @ York. Summer: M–Sun 10–8. Winter: (call to verify) M–Sun 11–6. www.harbourfront.on.ca

Health Haven

5555 Eglinton Ave. W. 621-3636. This award-winning vegan vegetarian restaurant offers pampering table service in a cozy relaxing dining atmosphere. Wholesaling and catering services available.Eglinton @ Dixie. M–W 11–7, Th–Sat 11–9. www.healthhavenfoods.com

Heart Lake Conservation Area

10818 Heart Lake Rd. 667-6299. Home of fishing derbies in spring/summer and Heart Lake Fall Festival, Heart Lake's dense forests make you feel like you're hours from the city. This conservation area also has great fishing and canoeing. A nature retreat. Hwy 7 @ Hwy 10. 9–dusk (spring–fall). www.trca.on.ca/4ag.html

Hotel Employees, Restaurant Employees Union, Local 75

229 Yonge, Ste 502. 216-0875. Toronto's largest union in the tourism industry. Active participants in the Green Tourism Association and other tourism organizations in Toronto. Yonge @ Queen. 9–4:30.

Hostelling International

76 Church 971-4440. Offers inexpensive accommodation to travellers of all ages. Members, non-members and groups welcome. Shared and family rooms are available. Church @ King. 24 hours. www.hostellingint-gl.on.ca

Humber Arboretum

205 Humber College Blvd. 675-5009. A jewel in the Toronto landscape; enjoy the beautiful gardens or explore the surrounding woodlots, meadows, and wetlands.Hwy 27 @ Humber College Blvd. Open sunup to sundown.

Humber College - HRT Alliance

205 Humber College Blvd. 675-6622 ext. 5012. Humber College Eco & Adventure Tourism certificate program. A 1-1/2 year full-time program offering the opportunity to grow with this exciting industry. Hwy 27 @ Humber College Blvd. Summer: 9–5. Winter: 8–5. www.hrtalliance.com

Indian Line Campground

7625 Finch Ave. W. 905-678-1233 or 1-800-304-9728 (call to confirm open days). This tourist campground can offer you an on-the-lake holiday right inside Toronto. You can camp, swim, fish and canoe while being close to Toronto's best attractions. Finch Ave. @ Hwy 427. www.trca.on.ca/4ad.html

Karma Food Co-op

739 Palmerston Ave. 534-1470. A non-profit food store, owned co-operatively by the people who shop there - its members. Treats include free range eggs, bulk grains and organic meats. Near Bloor @ Bathurst. M 12–7, Tu–Th 12–9, F 10–9, Sat 10–6, Sun 11–5.

Kluane's Creations

364-4912 (call ahead). A unique greeting gift/card and herb kit all in one. The all-Canadian seeds are organic and secured to little pots in a Victorian method. These gifts give everyone with a passion for nature, cooking and herbs, their own fresh Victorian herb experience! Gift cards are available at Arts on King, Edwards Gardens and Royal Botanical Gardens. www.goodlife.com

Kortright Centre for Conservation and Centre for Sustainable Living

9550 Pine Valley Dr. 905-832-2289. With more than 15 km of trails on 162 hectares of forests, meadows and wetlands, Kortright is a nature enthusiast's dream come true. Learn about maple syrup, flora and fauna, and renewable energy from their experts. Toronto Region Conservation Authority managed and operated. Well signed from Hwy 400 N and Major MacKenzie Dr. 10–4. www.kortright.org

The Lambton House (Heritage York)

4066 Old Dundas 767-5472. 150 year-old Lambton House (national historic site) is the only remaining public building of historic Lambton Mills on the East bank of the Humber River. It was home to Sir William Pierce Howland, a Father of Confederation. Near Dundas @ Jane. Summer: Sat 10–2. Winter: Sat 10–12, or by appointment.

Le Commensal Fine Vegetarian Cuisine

655 Bay (entrance on Elm) 596-9364. Discover delicious vegetarian cuisine from the traditional to the exotic, all available at a hot, cold, and dessert buffet. Pay-by-weight. Inquire about free parking. French country kitchen and serene ambience. Bay @ Dundas. 11:30–10. www.toronto.com/lecommensal

Les Amis Vegetarian Bed & Breakfast

31 Granby 591-0635. Open year-round. A green bed & breakfast from France right in the city centre. Hot vegetarian breakfast. Yonge @ Carlton. www.bbtoronto.com

Mackenzie House

82 Bond 392-6915. This restored Greek-revival townhouse was the last home of William Lyon Mackenzie - politician, journalist, rebel, and Toronto's first mayor. Near Yonge @ Dundas. Jan–Apr: S&S 12–5. May–Aug: Tu–Sun 12–5. Sept–Dec: Tu–F 12–4 S&S 12–5. www.city.toronto.on.ca/culture

Marigold International Travellers Hostel

2011 Dundas W. 536-8824. We provide mostly dormitory rooms for budget travellers - no membership needed. Coin lockers available, linen provided and free coffee. Travellers of all ages welcome. Dundas W @ Howard Park. 24 hours; Check-in after 2pm.

Market Gallery

95 Front E. 392-7604. A public exhibition facility located in Toronto's 19th Century city council chamber, today enclosed in South St. Lawrence Market. Themed exhibitions of archives, art, and community displays use photographs and maps to explore facets of Toronto history. Front E @ Jarvis. W–F 10–4, Sat 9–4, Sun 12–4.

McBride Cycle Harbourfront Rentals

180 Queens Quay W. 763-5651. Toronto's quality bicycle repairs and rentals. Rents triathlon-level racing bikes, full suspension mountain bikes and everything in between. Queens Quay W @ York.

Mimico Hostel and Bed & Breakfast

150 Queens Ave. 251-6208. Non-smoking Home Hostel and Bed & Breakfast in SW Toronto. Shared and private rooms available. Major credit cards accepted. Call first for reservation. Near Royal York @ Lakeshore. 9–9. http://home.ican.net/~derekb/

Montgomery's Inn

4709 Dundas W. 394-8113. Now restored as a living museum to the 1847–50 period, the inn's costumed historical interpreters create the feeling of being at an inn long ago.Dundas W.@ Islington. Tu–F 9:30–4:30, S&S 1–5. www.montgomerysinn.com

More Than Just Walking

701-1515. An opportunity to explore new places in various parks around the Greater Toronto Area while meeting new and interesting people in a healthy environment. Year round. http://members.home.net/walking

Mountain Equipment Co-op

400 King W. 340-2667. Mountain Equipment Co-op is a member-owned and directed retail consumer co-operative which provides products and services for wilderness activities in an environmentally responsible manner. King @Spadina. M–W 10–7, Th–F 10–9, Sat 9–6, Sun 11–5. www.mec.ca

Mount Pleasant Cemetery

375 Mount Pleasant Rd. 485-9129. With more than 200 species of trees and shrubs, Mount Pleasant Cemetery, established in 1876, has one of the finest arboreta in North America. As the final resting place of many prominent Canadians, it is custodian of some of our nation's most fascinating history. Mount Pleasant @ Merton. 8am–1/2 hr before sunset.

Moving the Economy

388-5088. An evolving partnership dedicated to growing Toronto's susainable transportation sector by promoting and developing economic oportunities and innovations in sustainable transportation. www.city.toronto.on.ca/mte

Museum for Textiles

55 Centre Ave. 599-5321 or 599-2234. The only museum in Canada exclusively devoted to the collection, exhibition and documentation of textiles from around the world. In fiberspace, the visitor can explore the cultural and historical significance of the art form. The museum features continually changing exhibitions, lectures, workshops and other special events. Near Dundas W.@ University. M, Th, F 11–5, W 11–8, S&S 12–5. www.museumfortextiles.on.ca

Neill-Wycik College Hotel

96 Gerrard E. 977-2320. 300-room student residence offers clean, affordable accommodation in downtown Toronto. The only alternative to a regular hotel! College subway. Gerrard E. @ Church Summer: 24 hours in summer. Winter: 9–5. www.neill-wycik.com

Ontario Science Centre

Ⓣ

770 Don Mills Rd. 696-1000. Excites curiosity about science and technology through 800 exhibits and wide-ranging programs on everything from a hair-raising electrical generator to tracing your DNA fingerprints. Don Mills @ Eglinton. 10–5. www.osc.on.ca

People & Planet Friendly Events and Resources

Ⓣ

Planet-friendly events! Free weekly email newsletter and website. Green festivals, talks, films, broadcasts, courses, conferences, resources, opportunities, and links. www.web.ca/~ppf

Petticoat Creek Conservation Area

(partial)

1100 Whites Rd. 667-6299. Petticoat Creek has an incredible view from the bluffs along Lake Ontario on the Waterfront Trail, a pool larger than a football field, and an extraordinary owl nesting area. Whites Rd. @ Hwy 2. 1km S of Hwy 401. 9–dusk (spring–fall). www.trca.on.ca/4ah.html

Pine Hills Cemetery

Ⓣ

625 Birchmount Rd. 267-8229. More than 17,000 trees and shrubs were planted as part of the extensive landscaping programme undertaken when Pine Hills Cemetery was established in 1982. The addition of a wide variety of birds and other small wildlife make this a nature lover's paradise. St. ClairE.@ Birchmount. 8am–1/2 hr before sunset.

Prospect Cemetery

1450 St. Clair Ave. W. 651-4040. Fourteen stained-glass windows in the Court Mausoleum, and a superb tree collection which includes a Silver Maple planted in 1919 by HRH the Prince of Wales, are just two of the magnificent features of historic Prospect Cemetery. St. Clair W @ Lansdowne. 8am–1/2 hr before sunset.

Set Me Free Recycle Bike Company (Queen)

2130 Queen E. 698-3756. Carries a large selection of used and new bikes to suit all budgets. Bike rentals, service, parts and accessories are also available. Queen E between Woodbine & Victoria Park. M–F 11–7, Sat 10–6, Sun 12–5. Closed M in winter.

Set Me Free Recycle Bike Company (Roncesvalles)

381 Roncevalles Ave. 532-4147. Carries a large selection of used and new bikes to suit all budgets. Bike rentals, service, parts and accessories are also available. Near Bloor W @ Dundas W. M–F 11–7, Sat 10–6, Sun 12–5. Closed M in winter.

Riverdale Community Business Centre

1007 Gerrard E. 462-0496. The centre provides information on the wealth of bike paths, parks, green businesses, galleries and walking tours that make Riverdale a unique green destination. Gerrard @ Queen. M–F 9–5. www.riverdale.org

ROM Walks

100 Queen's Park Circle. 586-5513. A volunteer organization of the Royal Ontario Museum which conducts historical and architectural walks of various districts in the City of Toronto. Look for the distinctive blue umbrella! Museum subway. Queen's Park Circle @ Bloor Summer and winter walks available, call to inquire.

Rouge Park

50 Bloomington Rd. W., Aurora. 905-713-6007 (call ahead). North America's largest natural and cultural heritage park in an urban setting. Port Union Rd. @ Hwy. 2. www.rougepark.com

Ryerson Polytechnic University Conference Services

160 Mutual, Ste 101. 979-5296. Ryerson Polytechnic University offers affordable accommodation and 50 different meeting spaces in an environment conducive to learning in downtown Toronto. Near Gerrard E @ Church. 24 hours, May to Aug. www.ryerson.ca

Scarborough Historical Museum

(partial)

1007 Brimley Rd. 431-3441. From an early settlers cabin to a rural Victorian home, experience life as it was in 19th-century Scarborough. Brimley @ Lawrence E. Summer: W–Sun 12–4. Spring & Fall: M–F 10–4.

Sephiroth Health Store and Juice Bar

898 Queen E. 461-4612. Health food store and juice bar supporting environmental programs and the local economy. Queen E @ Logan . Summer: M–F 8–9, S&S 10–6. Winter: M–W 8–6, Th–F 8–9, Sat 10–5, Sun 11–5. www.sephiroth.on.ca

Sir Sandford Fleming College

Haliburton Campus offers ecotourism and adventure tourism programs. www.flemingc.on.ca

Skyland Tours

234 Eglinton Ave. E, Ste 407. 545-1993. An inbound tour operator for Japanese tourists. www.skyland.com

Spadina Historic House and Gardens

285 Spadina Rd. 392-6910. An elegant museum with six acres of parkland, has some of Toronto's finest restored Victorian and Edwardian Gardens. Spadina @ Davenport. Jan-Apr: S&S 12–4. May–Dec: Tu–Sun 12–5. Call to confirm opening hours. www.torontohistory.on.ca

Steam Whistle Brewing Inc.

255 Bremner Blvd. 362-2337. This micro-brewery is located in a national historic site offering daily tours and tasting of the brewery's premium European pilsner. Union subway, behind the C.N. Tower. Near Spadina @ Lakeshore. Summer: 12–7. Winter: 12–2. www.steamwhistle.ca

Sutton Place

955 Bay 924-9221. A downtown luxury hotel located in the heart of the city and suitable for both business and social schedules. Leisure travelers appreciate the location near the Royal Ontario Museum, trend-setting Yorkville shops, the Toronto Eaton Centre and an array of excellent restaurants. Bay @ Wellesley. www.suttonplace.com

The Pier and Toronto's Waterfront Museum

245 Queens Quay W. 338-7437. The Pier invites you to discover the exciting story of Toronto's waterfront from the last ice age to the present. Queens Quay W @ Rees. Jul–Aug: 10–6. Sept, Oct, Mar, Apr, May: 10–4.

Todmorden Mills Heritage Museum and Arts Centre

Pottery Rd. between Broadview Ave. and Bayview Ave. 396-2819. This 200 year-old site was once a thriving industrial community with homes, mills and a brewery. Visitors explore two historic homes, galleries and a wildflower preserve. May Sept: Tu–F 11–4:30, Wknds 12–5. Oct–Dec: M–F 10–4. www.city.toronto.on.ca/todmorden

Toronto & Region Conservation Authority (TRCA)

5 Shoreham Dr. 661-6600. A not-for-profit provincial/municipal partnership devoted to the protection, enhancement, and public enjoyment of the environment by providing outdoor recreation opportunities, sound environmental information and advice, world class conservation education and heritage programs within the Greater Toronto Area. Sites in Toronto: Black Creek Pioneer Village, Indian Line Campground, Kortright Centre for Conservation, Tommy Thompson Park. Conservation Areas: Albion Hills, Boyd, Bruce's Mill, Glen Haffy, Heart Lake, Petticoat Creek. M–F 8:30–4:30. www.trca.on.ca

Tommy Thompson Park (Leslie Street Spit)

Leslie and Lakeshore Ave. 667-6299. Canada's largest constructed peninsula, the park is a significant stop-over for migratory birds and a designated Important Bird Area (IBA). A favorite place to enjoy cycling, walking and nature appreciation. Open to the public on weekends with a transit connection via bus or shuttle. www.trca.on.ca/ttp.html

Toronto Cycling Committee

392-7592. The Toronto Cycling Committee is a volunteer organization that advises City Council and City departments on the design, development and delivery of bicycle policies, programs and facilities to promote and enhance cycling in Toronto. www.city.toronto.on.ca/cycling

Toronto Historical Association

An umbrella organization representing more than 60 museums, historical sites, heritage organizations and historical societies involved in Toronto's natural, built and cultural heritage. www.tha.on.ca

The Toronto Necropolis and Crematorium

200 Winchester 923-7911. The Toronto Necropolis, established in 1850, is the final resting place of many of Toronto's fascinating pioneers, and is home to many beautiful trees. The Chapel is one of the finest examples of High Victorian Gothic architecture in Toronto. Castle Frank subway or Parliament bus. Winchester @ Parliament 8am–1/2 hour before sunset.

Tourism Environment

532-1641. Consultants in strategic planning and marketing for tourism.

Tourism Toronto

207 Queen's Quay W. 203-2500 or 1-800-363-1990. Promotion of tourism in Toronto. Harbourfront streetcar from Union Station. M–F 8:30–5:30, S&S 9–5. www.tourism-toronto.com

Travel by Rail

701-0756. More to do, more to see, new friends to meet. Visit the cyber-rail office, join the club - put your dreams on track. Market consulting services are also available. Tours can be arranged. Reservation line open 24 hours a day. www.travelbyrail.com

West Toronto Junction Historical Society

145 Annette 763-3161. This heritage organization for the Junction neighbourhood hosts walking tours and programs and participates in community events. West Toronto Junction Historical Society also publishes quarterly newsletters and maintains archives. Call first. M 3–5, Th 6–8. www.junctionhistory.on.ca

Wheel Excitement Inc.

5 Rees 260-9000. Toronto's foremost specialists of in-line skate and mountain bike rentals with a friendly and comfortable recreational environment. Let's get rolling! Near Spadina Ave. @ Queen's Quay W. Summer: 10–7. Closed Nov–Feb. www.wheelexcitment.com

York Cemetery

101 Senlac Rd. 221-3404. Flower beds, water features,magnificent trees, the historically significant 1850s Georgian-style Michael Shepard House, a Russian Grand Duchess and an NHL defenceman make York Cemetery well worth a visit. Near Yonge @ Sheppard. 8am–1/2 hr before sunset.

401 Richmond Ltd.

401 Richmond W. 595-5900. A renovated historic factory building housing 130 artists and entrepreneurs. Amenities: courtyard café, roof garden, children's early learning/daycare centre, newsletter. Won the 1999 Heritage Toronto Award. Richmond @ Spadina. 9–3. www.401richmond.net

The Green Tourism Association Team

GREEN TOURISM ASSOCIATION STAFF:

Anna Gibson Executive Director
Rachel Dodds Marketing & Business Development Manager
Justin Lafontaine Administrative Assistant

GREEN TOURISM ASSOCIATION BOARD OF DIRECTORS:

Joan Miles (President) Chair, Toronto Panel, Heritage Preservation Board; Past President, West Toronto Junction Historical Society
Marion Joppe (Vice President) President, Heritage Toronto & Professor, School of Hospitality & Tourism Management, Ryerson University
Kevin Currie (Secretary Treasurer) Owner, Wheel Excitement
Lynn Harrison Professor, School of Hospitality & Tourism Management, Ryerson University
Tony Lippa Vice President, Bed & Breakfast Association of Downtown Toronto
Shirley Lum Owner, A Taste of the World Neighbourhood Bicycle Tours and Walk Inc.
Louise Roberge Executive Director, Attractions Ontario
Lyle Thompson Supervisor, Environmental Affairs, Fairmont Hotels and Resorts
Sue Zielinski Director, Moving the Economy, and Transportation Planner, City of Toronto

Footnotes

1 Hall, Michael C. and weiler, Beth. 1992; 4–5. What's special about special Internet Tourism in Special internet Tourism.

2 Developing an Urban Ecotourism Strategy for Metropolitan Toronto, Blackstone Corporation, 1996

3 The Toronto Environmental Handbook, Key Publishers Company Ltd. June 1999, p. 23

4 Interview with Denis Denault (Co-ordinator, Poetry On The Way), June 2000

5 1987 report "Individual and Community Benefits of Public Transit Services and Facilities"

6 www.city.toronto.on.ca

7 Toronto Theatre Alliance, History of Theatre in Toronto, p. 1

8 Interview with Alan Kirschbaum, May 2000

9 www.cmhc-schl.gc.ca

10 Tourism Toronto, Fast Facts, 1998

11 Tourism Toronto: 1999 Visitors Guide, p. 5

12 Toronto Region Checklist of the Birds, Publications committee of the Ornithological Club, May 1996

13 Toronto Parkland Naturalization Update, Economic Development, Culture & Tourism Department, City of Toronto, 1999, p. 6

14 Toronto at the Crossroads, Shaping our Future, City of Toronto, p. 123

15 Western Ravine Discovery Walk brochure, Parks and Recreation division, City of Toronto

16 High Park — Oak Savannah brochure, Parks and Recreation division, City of Toronto

17 Toronto and Region Conservation Authority

18 Yvonne Yamoka, email 4/9/99

19 Toronto Parkland Naturalization Update, Economic Development, Culture & Tourism Department, City of Toronto, 1999, p. 6

20 www.city.toronto.on.ca

21 Interview with Jane Beecroft, August 2000

22 www.trca.on.ca

23 Eastern Ravine & beaches discovery Walk Brochure, Parks and Recreation, division, City of Toronto

24 www.trec.on.ca

25 Humber Discovery Walk brochure, Parks and Recreation division, City of Toronto

26 www.city.toronto.on.ca/parks/treeadvocacy.htm

27 Tourism Toronto, Fast Facts, 1998

28 The Toronto Environmental Handbook, Key Publishers Company Ltd. June 1999, p. 13

29 Christa Kroboth, A Stroll in the Park

30 The Toronto Environmental Handbook, Key Publishers Company Ltd. June 1999, p. 13

31 The Toronto Environmental Handbook, Key Publishers Company Ltd. June 1999, p. 13

32 Toronto Parkland Naturalization Update, Economic Development, Culture & Tourism Department, City of Toronto, 1999, p. 30

33 Interview with Alan Kirschbaum, May 2000, www.trca.on.ca, www.virtualbirder.com

Index

INDEX

How did we do?

We know that no matter how hard we tried there are going to be some cool green things in Toronto that we missed. Please drop us a line and let us know what you discover and any suggestions you may have so we can keep growing our information base!
greento@city.toronto.on.ca

Disclaimer: While this Guide book does not by any means intend to be exhaustive we hope it presents a vision of an other, greener way of exploring our city. Although we make every effort to provide accurate and reliable information, the Green Tourism Association, it's directors, members, and staff can not be held responsible for any errors or misrepresentations. Check our website for updated information.